PURE HEART

XXXchurch.com resource

PURE HEART

a woman's guide to sexual integrity

SHELLIE R. WARREN

BakerBooks

a division of Baker Publishing Group
Grand Rapids, Michigan

© 2010 by Fireproof Ministries

Published by Baker Books
a division of Baker Publishing Group
P.O. Box 6287, Grand Rapids, MI 49516-6287
www.bakerbooks.com

Printed in the United States of America

Library of Congress Cataloging-in-Publication Data
Warren, Shellie R., 1975–
    Pure heart : a woman's guide to sexual integrity / Shellie R. Warren.
       p.   cm. — (XXXchurch.com resource)
    Includes bibliographical references (p.   ).
    ISBN 978-0-8010-7207-9 (pbk.)
    1. Pornography—Religious aspects—Christianity. 2. Christian women—Religious life. 3. Chastity. I. Title.
    BV4597.6.W36 2010
    241′.66082—dc22   2010019050

XXXchurch.com is represented by Wheelhouse Literary Group, 1007 Loxley Drive, Nashville, TN 37211.

To protect the privacy of those whose stories are shared by the author, some names and details have been changed.

10   11   12   13   14   15   16   7   6   5   4   3   2   1

This book is dedicated to every young woman who doesn't understand the power of her purpose (yet) and to three princesses in particular whom I believe, in spite of the hands they were dealt, will change "the game" as we know it: Rochelle, Kristin Joyce, and Starkeisha. I see you. I'm praying. I got you.

To my goddaughter, Tasia Selah Mitchell. Thank you for providing the opportunity of a "do-over." I am both honored and thrilled. You amaze me every time I see you (or hear you).

To my "pro-life" baby, Caroline Irene Dye. Who knows what my life would have been like had I gotten "the call" before my abortions? Your mommy is such a warrior. *You are such a miracle.*

To the future children God will bless me with. You will be happy that this book came before you did . . . *trust me.*

And finally, if there was one verse to sum up this entire book, it would have to be Malachi 2:15: "God made husbands and wives to become one body and one spirit for his purpose—so they would have children who are true to God." I personally wish I had honored it much sooner. I pray that you will.

The greatest thing God ever made was a woman.

—Shannon Sanders,
Granny-winning
singer and songwriter

Contents

Foreword

Further and *faster*. These are the two words that come to mind when I think of porn use in today's culture. Porn will take a person further than they ever wanted to go and destroy their world faster than they ever thought possible.

When I started XXXchurch, I encountered so many people who were gripped by the addiction of porn. They had been entangled by the web and its seductive bait of the two-dimensional woman who would never say no. The majority, mostly men, had no idea how deep their depravity would take them. Few recognized their eyes would never be satisfied. That was the late 1990s.

Over a decade has passed, and we have seen the line blur between who is susceptible to porn and who is safe. No longer is porn a strictly male pastime. Women, in staggering proportions, are curiously diving headlong into blind addiction. They never expected it to grab them. In fact most were lured in through curiosity. Many slowly cracked open porn's Pandora's box to see what it was that had gripped their lover, husband, son, boyfriend, or pastor. They wanted to know who this mysterious lover was who lived only a few clicks away. As they sought to investigate, the isolation, the eye candy, the fantasy that flickered before them tickled an arousal that had never been awakened.

To counter this sad phenomenon, we have gathered experts, written curriculum, started accountability groups, and hoped and prayed for the best. In some cases we have been successful. In others we have missed the mark by a mile.

We knew we needed a book for women, and we knew it had to be written by a woman. Who better to understand a woman's journey than a woman? Who better to bring issues and solutions to the table than a woman? Who better to give hope and remedy to what seems to be an unbreakable addiction than someone who has lived on the frontlines of "further and faster"?

What you are holding is help. Maybe it is not you who needs help but someone you love. Either way, Shellie offers straightforward advice to women about how to retain or regain sexual purity—all drawn from the powerful combination of scriptural truth and practical experience. Her casual style of writing is reminiscent of a girls' night out. Her pragmatic solutions are blunt while still wrapped in compassion. If Oprah was ever to have a book club selection to speak to the heart of a woman's fight with sexual addictions, this would be it.

Read this book and allow God to apply it to your soul. Wholeness is within your reach.

Hopeful,
Craig Gross

The Letter That Got
This Book Started . . .

Dear Shellie,

I know you don't know me, but I have read a lot of your stuff and I feel like you might be able to relate. I don't want to share this with anyone that I know and, as weird as it may sound, sometimes it's easier telling a stranger what you've done than your best friend . . .

It's such a long story. Basically, I've slept with so many men that I've lost count and now my period is late. The worst part is that my parents don't even know that I'm having sex. I'm really active in my church and a lot of kids younger than I am look up to me.

I'm not sure why I can't stop having sex. I just don't really feel pretty without it. I don't know if that sounds weird to you or not, but even though I was raised as a Christian, I was never really told the *purpose* for sex or even why it was a good reason to wait. All I heard was that fornication was a sin, a sin that could send me to hell.

I already feel like I'm in hell. I currently don't have a boyfriend but I am involved with three different guys. I told two of them that my period was late and they haven't returned my phone calls. I'm lost. Can you help me?

I don't know where to begin.

In the Beginning . . .

In the beginning was the Word, and the Word was with God, and the Word was God.

John 1:1 NKJV

Life on the planet is born of woman.

Adrienne Rich, author and poet

For years, I've said that I wanted to get married on a Friday evening. The Lord knows we can't always get what we want, nor am I the only person who can make that decision (what's up with women planning weddings without the input of men, anyway?). For some reason, when I think about the *creation of marriage*, I just like the beauty and order of the creation week: man and woman made on the sixth day (see Gen. 1:26–31). I thought it would be cool to someday enter into the Sabbath (2:1–3) as a wife. Talk about a whole new level of rest . . . or unrest, depending on how you look at it. Either way, a blessed state to be in (I giggle just thinking about it!).

In 2004 I wrote what I call my "sex memoir": *Inside of Me: Lessons of Lust, Love and Redemption*. I call it a "sex memoir" because, like every person, there is so much more to me than my sex life. However, that doesn't mean that my sexuality is *any less important* than, say, my professional life, my family, or even my spirituality. As a matter of fact, one of the biggest disservices that I believe the church has done is to try to separate who we are as sexual beings from everything else about us—as if we are to just put our sexual needs on the shelf and dust them off once we say "I do." Being sexual is not a curse; however, to not understand the purpose behind our sexuality can be a curse if we're not careful. *Inside of Me*, the book that I lovingly refer to as my firstborn "creative" child, is something that I hold very near and dear to my heart. It is what my mother refers to as my "emotional throw up," and in many ways she is right. It helped me see where I had been in preparation for where I wanted to go. It candidly revealed what happens when you use something while having absolutely no idea what it's really meant for.

On so many levels the creation story seems like a great way to get back to what so many of us seem to have lost sight of: marriage, God's way. In the Garden, Adam and the Woman were as close to God as humanly possible. In the Garden, all of their needs were met. In the Garden, they were very clear about their purpose. And it's that last point that serves as the main focus of and purpose for this book.

This book? Prayerfully, it will pick up where *Inside of Me* left off—for both the writer and the reader—because the funny thing (not in the "ha-ha" but the "aha" kind of way) is that in the intro of my first book, I listed all of the reasons why sex outside of marriage was not a good idea. And all of them were dead-on. But it wasn't until 2007—that's right, *three years later*—that I actually stopped having sex for good. Well, until I get married, that is. Hey, I'm obedient, but I'm not a nun. Not by any stretch of the imagination (and I have a big imagination!). I mean, I got mad respect for the apostle

Paul, but I have *no desire* to be like him when it comes to his quest for singleness (1 Cor. 7:8). I love the single life, but not enough to be single (and celibate) forever.

So yes, that means I desire to be married. And when I do, I hope to remain so until death parts me from my mate. While sex is not the be-all of marriage (believe me, I've heard enough war stories to know), I did once hear a wise *married* man say that good marital sex is 10 percent of a marriage and bad marital sex is 90 percent of a marriage. The bedroom tends to set the tone for the rest of the house, whether married or single.

The Beginning . . . of It All

Sex isn't just about what we see on so-called reality television shows or our favorite romantic dramedies (thank the Lord!). Sex is about joining two human minds, bodies, *and* spirits together. It is one of the ultimate forms of communication between a man and a woman—ideally, husband and wife. The truth is, whomever you have sex with, you become joined to . . . forever. I once heard a man say that they don't pay prostitutes for sex; they pay them to leave. According to 1 Corinthians 6:15–16, that man was delusional. It may be by floss or it may be by tightly woven rope, but every single individual you have sex with, you become linked to from that moment forward. That is the main role sex plays: connector.

Sex is about joining two human minds, bodies, and spirits together.

Like so many women (and while I think men can benefit from reading this, I am writing to my spiritual sisters), I didn't really understand the true role of sex in life. My mom told me about the birds and the bees at a fairly young age, and my Christian educational upbringing pretty much beat into my head that sex outside of marriage is not something that "good girls" do. Looking back, I guess they meant *single* good girls, because aren't married women "good girls" too? (That was not a rhetorical question; we'll get to that in another chapter!) But even with all of the "book knowledge" I had on the issue, I still didn't really get the purpose of why God created sex or what he desired for his daughters to experience in that area.

And so, on my current quest for sexual fulfillment—from a spiritual perspective *first*—I figured why not go to the first woman documented in the Good Book? *The* Woman (she wasn't called "Eve" until after sin—Gen. 3:20). The Woman was *brought* to Adam. See that? As much as we quote this section of Scripture and say many a man may *find* a good wife (see Prov. 18:22), Adam didn't actually *find* his; he slept, while God planned his future (Gen. 2:21–22). Wonder what the experience was like for the Woman? How did she feel being created from a man and then seeing him for the first time? Well, I won't speak for her because I hate it when people speak for me, but if I were to put myself in her shoes, as a Word of Affirmation person (because you have read Gary Chapman's *The Five Languages of Love*, right?), if Adam had been *my* husband, he would have earned *major points* for praising me on seeing me: "And the man said, 'Now, this is someone whose bones came from my bones, whose body came from my body. I will call her "woman," because she was taken out of man'" (v. 23).

Okay, let's stop right here for a moment. Already we see something that many women miss when it comes to experiencing a romantic relationship with a man. It was when Adam was working (ladies, please get a man with a j-o-b!) that he realized that everyone had a partner but him (v. 20). There was a longing within him from the start. But it was God who began to put everything into action. God said it was not good for man to be alone, even before Adam started to realize that he didn't want to be by himself (v. 18). Then God put him to sleep so that the Big Guy could form what was missing in

Adam's life. It was then that God created her—the Woman. And what was her job description? Helper: a person who helps or gives assistance, support. "The man gave names to all the tame animals, to the birds in the sky and to all the wild animals. But Adam did not find a helper that was right for him" (v. 20).

What was the Woman's job description? Helper.

Oh, if we ladies just got that part of the love story down, I believe a lot of our love lives would run a lot smoother. We were created *to help*.

Help for the Helper

As women, this is a huge, *huge* part of our purpose on this earth—to provide assistance and support in every way. I know that a lot of you are in relationships right now and because of that fact, I want you to take a moment and ask yourself, *Am I helping him?* As a matter of fact, let me further qualify the question: *Am I helping* to better him? Not enabling, but helping? I know it's not mentioned very often, but ladies, do you realize just how much God thinks of you to have made you a woman? He thinks you are qualified to *help* others—especially your current or future covenant partner, handpicked by God.

The more I think about it, the more it blows my mind how inadequate we sometimes view ourselves to be, like we should have to beg, plead, manipulate, seduce, and settle below the standards God gives us, in order to gain a man's attention and affection. *The man needs us.* We're his help! I believe it is in accepting this biblically based fact that I can understand the following verse a lot more than I used to: "When a man finds a wife, he finds something good. It shows that the LORD is pleased with him" (Prov. 18:22).

Let me stop right here too. I'm a writer by trade, and so it comes with the occupation to want to research—and in this case research and share—the definitions of words. A man "finding" you doesn't mean you create all kinds of crazy strategies for him to prove himself worthy. *Manipulating him is not helping him.* When it comes to a man finding us, we must free our minds from the definitions we've been told and spend some time on what the word actually means. Single ladies, the Bible says that the truth will make you free (John 8:32), and the truth is that there's a whole lot of ways your future husband can *find* you. He could:

- come upon you by chance
- meet you
- locate, attain, or obtain you by search or effort
- locate or recover you if you've been lost or misplaced
- discover or perceive you after consideration
- gain or regain the use of your help
- ascertain you by study or calculation
- feel or perceive your help
- become aware of you, as being in a condition or location
- discover you

What I get from this is that God is saying that a woman, a wife, however God brings the couple together, is worthy of being found. She is an excellent find. Yes, when the Woman was brought to Adam, she was immediately a blessing because she was to be a help to/for/with him.

God knew it. Adam knew it. Satan knew it.

Knowing the Enemy

I don't know how many of you are too "high-minded" to have checked out the movie *The Devil's Advocate* from back in the day, but it's one of my favorite films. There is a scene where Keanu Reeves's character and his wife, played by Charlize Theron, are at a party and the wife says (paraphrasing a bit), "Just don't let go of my hand." He assures her that he won't, but the Enemy immediately comes in to separate them (John 10:10). That's nothing new. When my girlfriends tell me about some jerk whistling at them on the street, I tell them, "It may be annoying, but he wouldn't do it if it hadn't worked before." We all tend to be creatures of habit. The Enemy (which is how I refer to Satan or the devil and pretty much will throughout the entire book) is very much the same way. What the screenwriter of *The Devil's Advocate* wrote is *exactly* what is documented in the Bible. In Genesis the Woman was instructed to help her man, and the Enemy immediately started working on a scheme that would entice *her* attention away from her purpose, not just of helping her husband but of obeying her Father: "The LORD God put the man in the garden of Eden to care for it and work it. The LORD God commanded him, 'You may eat the fruit from any tree in the garden, but you must not eat the fruit from the tree which gives the knowledge of good and evil. If you ever eat fruit from that tree, you will die!'" (Gen. 2:15–17).

The Enemy worked on a scheme that would entice her attention away from her purpose.

And how did the Enemy manage to make the Woman forget her purpose? By causing her to question it:

> Now the snake was the most clever of all the wild animals the LORD God had made. One day the snake said to the woman, "Did God really say that you must not eat fruit from any tree in the garden?"
> The woman answered the snake, "We may eat fruit from the trees in the garden. But God told us, 'You must not eat

fruit from the tree that is in the middle of the garden. You must not even touch it, or you will die.'"

But the snake said to the woman, "You will not die. God knows that if you eat the fruit from that tree, you will learn about good and evil and you will be like God!"

Genesis 3:1–5

Let's pause and ponder two points in these few verses of Scripture. The Bible says the snake is most *clever*. That means he was mentally bright, skillful, and witty. It also means he had some originality in his approach, which would make sense being that this was the first recorded sin on earth. My point? We cannot fight the Enemy (and win) on our own and we shouldn't even try. When Paul said in Philippians 4:13 that he could do all things, he didn't stop there. It's only *through Christ*, who gives him the strength, that he finds power. You think you can walk the road of sexual purity alone? You can't. And don't even let the Enemy try to tell you otherwise.

When God gives us an instruction (see 2 Tim. 3:16), and we find a questioning of it within ourselves, we can be assured the Enemy's spirit has come on us. From my perception, what got the Woman into the most trouble was attempting to defend and rationalize what she already knew—*to someone she didn't know*. I'm not judging her, because I can relate. Over my adult years especially, you have no idea how much trouble I have found myself in from doing the exact same thing. God tells me to wait until marriage before having sex (Eph. 5:2–4), for instance, and after a few dates a guy will say, "But aren't you attracted to me?"; "Are you actually going to wait until you're married?"; "Everybody's having sex. How are you going to know if we're sexually compatible without trying?" *That is the spirit of the serpent, the snake, the Enemy talking!* The moment I try to defend my stance, like the Woman, I am at risk of touching the forbidden fruit.

When I was catching some heat for the candor of my first book (which doesn't come close to where we are going with this one!), I recalled my mom saying to me, "Christ didn't defend himself, so don't you start doing it." Ladies, when the Word says that the One who is in us is greater than the one in the world (1 John 4:4), that is not meant to be some kind of "feel good Scripture." This means that when God tells us to do something, we aren't alone in fighting the battle to honor his Word.

> *The One who is in us is greater than the one in the world.*

It's when we believe otherwise that we find ourselves having "woman issues."

The story in Genesis goes on to say that when the Enemy told the Woman that what God said wasn't true, three things happened: "The woman *saw that the tree was beautiful, that its fruit was good to eat,* and *that it would make her wise.* So she took some of its fruit and ate it. She also gave some of the fruit to her husband who was with her, and he ate it" (Gen. 3:6).

Let's piece this apart:

1. The woman saw that the tree was beautiful.

Beauty—the first stumbling block. Follow me here. Actor Idris Elba. Know him? If you don't know him, look him up; he's beautiful. Matthew McConaughey? He's no slouch, either. But here's something I bet you haven't put a whole lot of thought into: when the Enemy was made, he was considered to be the most beautiful creature (Ezek. 27:4)! Now, I don't see anything wrong with a fine man, and should God bless you with one, well, God bless you. But make sure that it's God who is blessing you with what catches your eye. Certainly everything that glitters is not gold. The tree was beautiful to the eye, but it was also the haven of death.

2. The woman saw that the fruit was good to eat.

Let me tell you why I love this line so much. So many times, when I've been caught in my sin, either because I was literally caught or because I shared it in a testimony, people would say, "What were you thinking?" Good question. At the time I was thinking it would be the best thing for me because that is what I wanted to do. A very sad part of my testimony is that I have aborted four children. On the front end, yes, from both a biblical and moral perspective, I knew it was wrong. The sixth commandment clearly states we should not kill, and Jeremiah 1:5 clearly says that God knows us and our purpose *before the womb*. So yes, at conception, there is life, because *before* conception God had a plan for that life.

But after I found out that I was pregnant, the Enemy presented some interesting questions:

- How are you going to take care of a baby?
- What is your family going to say?
- Do you want to be tied to that man for the rest of your life?

Just like he did to the Woman at the tree, he presented a "fruit option" that seemed good at the time. And so I ate it. And like the Woman, my eyes were opened—partially—to things God never intended me to see, like the extreme pain and brokenness of abortion(s) and my having sex with people I was not married to.

What I also appreciate about this part of Eve's story is that it doesn't say she ate it and it was nasty. She ate of the fruit . . . and it was good. I'm going to be honest here. (You may not want to put your business out on the street, and perhaps that's why God assigned me to do this particular book instead of you.) Rarely, in the physical sense, have I experienced some "bad sex." When it came to how it pleased my flesh, it was like Campbell's soup: mmm, mmm, good. Still, it almost killed me—mind, body, and spirit. The things God warns us to stay away from, oftentimes it's not because they aren't good; *it's just that they're not good for us.* Sure, for the Woman, the fruit tasted good, but physical sensation came with a price—the price of her life and the break in oneness from Adam, whom she had been created to help.

3. *The woman saw that it would make her wise.*

This right here knocked me over like a ton of bricks. If you don't get anything else out of this chapter, please let this point resonate within you. For years I have been taught, from the pulpit and the media, that the Woman ate of the fruit because she was basically selfish. God told her not to. She wanted to. So she did. After reading this again and praying, I don't believe it's that simple, and when it comes to succumbing to sin, it rarely is. Again, the Woman was created to be a helper, right? Well, according to the Scriptures, the Enemy told her that eating the fruit *would help her.* She took the fruit thinking it would make her wiser, and she gave it to her husband believing it would make him wiser as well. *She thought she was helping.* She messed up, not in her intentions, *but in not following the initial directions.* God told her not to eat of the fruit of that tree, period. That meant, no matter what, that tree was not an option. Even in spite of what her motive may have been, her mistake was letting someone talk her out of what God told her to do. I can only be so mad at her because I've been duped as well:

- Not giving my tithe so I could cover the rent (Mal. 3:8–10)
- Making promises that I know I can't keep just to get someone off my back (Matt. 5:37)
- Telling someone's business to illustrate a point when I am to mind my own business (1 Thess. 4:11)

The intentions may be somewhat good, but I did not follow the directions that were given, the directions that are given to us all in the Word of God. That is what the Woman did that was so wrong. She didn't give the fruit to trick Adam. I believe she really believed it would assist, support, and help him. When you prioritize anything before God, it never works out the way you think it will or should.

One of my all-time favorite authors, Myles Monroe, once wrote that one of the biggest challenges in this life is deciphering the difference between doing what is good and what is right. God called us to do the latter. Had Christ come to this earth to be a carpenter only and not our Savior, he may have ended up doing a lot of *good*, but that is not why he was sent. To die for our sins is what was *right*. The Woman may have thought that what she was doing was good (becoming wise), but in taking the fruit . . . Who am I kidding? In simply hanging around the tree, she was not doing what was *right*. Right is doing what God told you to do. No more, no less.

> *Right is doing what God told you to do. No more, no less.*

Naked and Ashamed . . . or Not?

The story goes on to say that after eating the fruit, Adam and the Woman's eyes were opened. They realized they were naked (exposed) and needed to cover themselves. However, the biggest sign that something had gone wrong was that they heard God, their Creator, their Father, the Being who blessed them with the Garden and with each other. But instead of greeting the Almighty with open arms—*they hid* (Gen. 3:7–8). From that point on they began to experience emotions and consequences that God never desired for them:

> Then they heard the LORD God walking in the garden during the cool part of the day, and the man and his wife hid from

the LORD God among the trees in the garden. But the LORD God called to the man and said, "Where are you?"

The man answered, "I heard you walking in the garden, and I was afraid because I was naked, so I hid."

God asked, "Who told you that you were *naked*? Did you eat fruit from the tree from which I commanded you not to eat?"

The man said, "You gave this woman to me and she gave me fruit from the tree, so I ate it."

Then the LORD God said to the woman, "How could you have done such a thing?"

She answered, "The snake tricked me, so I ate the fruit."

Genesis 3:8–13

God never wanted any of us to be afraid of him. He never designed for us to feel naked and ashamed. As a matter of fact, he wanted just the opposite for us, to be naked and unashamed (Gen. 2:25). God never wanted us in positions where the Enemy would trick us. That is why he established clear rules for us. God created Lucifer and knows what will become of him—and God doesn't desire that kind of fate for his children. Not only that, but God doesn't just know the end from the beginning. Revelation 21:6 says that he *is* the end from the beginning. God knows all and sees all, and because he is also our Creator, he knows what the Enemy will use to try to seduce us away from the good plans God has for our lives (see Jer. 29:11).

I can only imagine how the Woman must have felt after all the curses were dealt out. She and the Enemy would now forever be at odds with one another, and not just her but all of her descendants (including you and me) to follow. People were actually going to have an enemy from birth all because of a choice she made (Gen. 3:15). Now, bringing life into the world was going to be painful. And not only that, but she would also have to submit to her husband (v. 16). Yes, if you read the story in its entirety, submission was a *consequence* for sin.

Okay, let me stop here for a moment. I know that submission often catches a bad rap and perhaps this is a part of the reason. We don't just serve a God who is loving (1 John 4:8), we serve a God who is also systematic in his approach, especially when it comes to the restoration. The Woman was tricked by the snake, right? The Bible is not really clear on how far apart she and Adam were when she was engaging the Enemy, but either way she wasn't much help to her husband by giving him a piece of forbidden fruit. Therefore, can you imagine how Adam must have felt after partaking of it, experiencing the nakedness and fear that came as a result, and then receiving the consequences? That's not to say that Adam doesn't need to take some responsibility in it all. God is not into tricking his children (that is what the Enemy is all about), and so I'm sure that something about the fruit seemed not "normal" even as he reached out to partake.

Adam also knew that he should put God and his instructions above all else, including his wife (a lesson unto itself). But either way the Woman was to help and when it came to this particular choice, she wasn't much help at all. My perspective? Putting her into a place of submission is actually God's way of protecting her on an elevated level. In this context one great definition of submission is "to present for the approval, consideration, or decision of another." I can only imagine how guilty she must have felt for doing what she did. God loved her enough to say, "I am going to provide a way for you to be covered. You will not have to make (major family) decisions by yourself. Consulting prayerfully with your mate will restore mutual trust, and he will be open to receiving your kind of help again."

Are you rolling your eyes? I admit this is often not the way that submission is taught, but I don't see anything in the Bible that would refute this theoretical approach. Just take a moment to think about the possible thoughts that ran through

Adam's mind when he went from having dominion over the Garden to having to sweat and toil for even his basic needs to be met (Gen. 3:17–19). Not only that, can you imagine being created to live forever and then being told that because you put your wife's suggestion above God's instruction, you would now die? Yeah, I don't know a man who wouldn't be more than a little heated about that.

Hmph. Perhaps that's a big part of the reason his helper's name went from Woman to Eve. Once she came under his submission, he preferred to call her "the mother of all the living" rather than "because you were taken out of man." Hmph, again. I can't help but wonder if there was a part of Adam that didn't want to be reminded that she was a part of him. And maybe, just maybe, that's where a lot of the drama between man and woman truly began. Drama that we still see today. I can see men asking themselves, *Have a woman for what? At the end of the day, she's just going to curse me.* And if that is how Adam felt, can you imagine what it must have been like to live around that kind of emotional energy? Now I'm not saying Adam didn't still love Eve, but it goes without saying that unconditional trust was severely broken, and in many ways it seems like men and women are still trying to figure out how to get it back.(Yeah, Adam and the men to follow may be upset, but they're obviously not mad enough to stop sleeping with us. So true.)

As I was continuing through the story of Adam and (now) Eve, I found it fascinating that right after God *forced* them out of the Garden (Gen. 3:24) so that they could not get access to the Tree of Life, the very next line of the story says the following: "*Adam had sexual relations with his wife Eve*, and she became pregnant and gave birth to Cain. Eve said, 'With the Lord's help, I have given birth to a man'" (4:1).

Even with the pain, even with the relational trauma, even with the curses and consequences, they still had sex. Except on this side of the Garden, it was sex with sin attached. Now they were naked with a stench of shame.

The bottom line of why we see a lot of the filth that goes on in society as it relates to sex is because there is generational shame attached to it. Sex was designed to bring oneness to people, and when it came to Adam and Eve, now Adam's anger was "one" with Eve's remorse. His resentment was "one" with Eve's fear. His pain was "one" with Eve's distress. The blessing of sex within the Garden of Eden was that Adam and the Woman were naked and *not* ashamed. Now, on this side of their choices, there is a ton of disgrace and regret, ridicule and disapproval attached to the experience. Physically, for so many of us, there is still pleasure in the act, but there is also a measure of this baggage within many marriages.

Whenever I speak on sex, I share my belief that two of the greatest threats to the Enemy were two of God's greatest gifts in the Garden: the seventh-day Sabbath (2:2–3) and sex (vv. 24–25). Few of us see the beauty in resting on the day that God blessed and hallowed (Exod. 20:8–11), and many of us are losing sight of the purpose of spiritual, physical, relational oneness. The Enemy knows far too well the benefits that come with both. When it comes to oneness, a benefit that sexual intercourse provides, Deuteronomy 32:30 tells us that two people joined have the ability to put as many as ten thousand to flight. Matthew 18:19–20 holds the promise that if two agree on anything that they ask, God will do it for them. Matthew 19:6 says that what God has joined together, no man should separate. The Message version of 1 Corinthians 6:16 states that "sex is as much spiritual mystery as physical fact." Sex holds a lot of power and God made it that way. The Enemy has been out to destroy it, in any way he can, ever since.

> *Sex was designed to bring oneness to people.*

A wise man once said that you must know where you've been to know where you're going. When God said that Eve's descendants would suffer, he meant what he said.

God told *Abraham and Sarah* they would have a son. Sarah didn't fully believe God (obviously—she was ninety!), and so she instructed her husband to have sex with one of her slave girls, Hagar. Sin encouraged mankind to have sex outside of covenant (Genesis 16).

When God told *Lot* to leave Sodom and Gomorrah because of how sinful the city had become, he and his two daughters found themselves in a cave. Fearful that they would never get a man of their own, they decided to get their father drunk and sleep with him so they could become pregnant. Sin encouraged mankind to be impatient and to commit incest (19:30–38).

When *Jacob* saw Rachel, whom he loved and desired to marry, he set out to work for her. Rachel's father, Jacob's uncle Laban, had other ideas and tricked Jacob into marrying his older daughter, Leah, first. Then Jacob had to continue to work for the woman he really wanted. Sin encouraged mankind to be competitive and resentful, even when it comes to sexuality (29:15–30:24).

When *Dinah*, Jacob's daughter, went to visit some friends, Shechem, the son of the ruler Hamor, raped Dinah and then had the nerve to fall in love with her and attempt to marry her. Sin encouraged mankind to confuse love with lust (Genesis 34).

Samson. Where do we begin? He was told not to be unequally yoked with the Philistines, the very people he was commissioned to defeat. He didn't listen. While on the way to Gaza, Samson slept with a prostitute, Delilah, and then was overcome by her. Sin encouraged mankind to ignore God's purpose (Judges 13–16).

David saw a beautiful woman. He wanted her, although she was another's wife. David didn't care. He let his desire consume him. That desire led to years of death and sorrow. Sin encouraged mankind to break godly order and defile the covenant of marriage (2 Samuel 11).

God told *Hosea* to marry the prostitute Gomer. If you have never read Francine Rivers's book *Redeeming Love*, I promise you it's a worthwhile investment that will change your life forever. Sin encouraged mankind, especially womankind, to become so broken that they would peddle their flesh instead of choosing to nurture their soul.

Now do you see the domino effect of the Woman's decision? Are you better able to understand what God was trying to spare us from, even sexually? The rest of this book will fast-forward thousands of years to where we are today—to how God's Word still rings true, how sin has continued to tear apart what is intended to be a sacred and special gift, and how, if you are willing, sex can be restored in your life to the special gift it was meant to be.

Sex in Purpose

- - - - - - - - - - -

"I love that I waited until marriage. There is trust between me and my husband that I don't think would have been there had we not. I can rely on his protection because even in our courtship, I watched how he put God above all else. It's not that it was easy to wait, it's that we wanted to be obedient. We put faith in God's Word that he would honor our marriage if we did, and he has. My wedding day and wedding night were some of the most beautiful memories I've ever had. To spend the rest of your life with a man, without the memories of other men haunting and/or taunting you, makes the love journey so liberating. It is always better to obey than to sacrifice."

Rachel Hockett, author, actress, singer

Sex Out of Purpose

- - - - - - - - - - -

"I've hit rock bottom! I have dated a man who was married in the beginning and now separated with children. He doesn't let me break up with him. . . . I try and then he starts getting upset and I know what I am doing isn't right. . . . Because of our situation I was pregnant a little over a year ago and had to have an abortion. I still haven't gotten over it and am in the process of getting over a lot of things in life that I have and am doing that aren't right."

Roxy Grl, XXXchurch.com women's blog reader

Sex

In and Out of Purpose

And they were both naked, the man and his wife, and were not ashamed.

Genesis 2:25 NKJV

Intimacy is being seen and known as the person you truly are.

Amy Bloom, author

This morning I was talking to my friend about an odd and ironic experience that I had over the weekend. I was meeting up with one of my engaged girlfriends and her family at a bridal shop for our bridesmaid dress fitting. Now, I'll be honest with you, I am fed up with being the "tail" and not the "head" side of the word *bridesmaid*. It's not that I am jealous of my friends. It's just that I too long for the day when

I will be able to prepare for my *prince*, the word my mother uses to describe my future husband.

As I was driving in a thunderstorm crying out, "Why, God, why?" and "When, God, when?" do you know what he revealed to me? That this book is part of my preparation. Throughout my journey of writing, you will probably see John 8:32— "You shall know the truth and the truth will make you free" (NKJV)—repeated more than just about any other Scripture. Time, experience, and observation have shown me that *the truth* is, a lot of women are not concerned with becoming *a wife* so much as becoming *a bride*. A lot of us want to set bridal shop appointments but don't want to set up any premarital counseling sessions. A lot of us are more consumed with the dress we want to wear than the cross we'll have to bear (obedience to God and submission to mate—Eph. 5:22). A lot of us desire the wedding day but not the covenant lifetime that is to follow. The truth? Every day we are obedient, even if we don't see a manifestation of what we desire, if it is within the will of God, it is a time of preparation.

Okay, God. I hear you.

So, anyway, as I was driving twenty miles away from where I live to get measured for another dress I probably won't wear again (unless to do an improv comedy sequel to *27 Dresses*, then I'm their girl!), I got a phone call from an unfamiliar number. When I picked it up, I heard a young girl's voice rambling. I figured she had the wrong number, told her so, and hung up the phone. About three minutes later, I got the call again. Again, she was rambling . . . and this time, yelling.

"Excuse me," I interjected. "I think you have *the wrong number.*"

She kept on talking. I was annoyed. Then God brought to my mind what it must be like for a lot of my friends when they are talking to me and *I* am not listening to them. Touché, God. I hung up again, but without as much of an attitude. If you are wondering how this is relevant to this chapter, I was just getting to that.

It was while I was trying on my strapless and surprisingly cute bridesmaid dress that I heard a beep on my cell phone letting me know that I had a text message. While in my dress and feeling as diva (in a good way) as ever, I checked it. The message included a desperate plea for a man's attention (obviously, it was again a wrong number). The texter practically begged for sex—using specific language, I might add.

On so many levels and for so many reasons, at least when it comes to my cell phone, that is not okay. But when I looked at the phone number, I realized it was from the same girl I had spoken with just moments before. This time, I called *her*.

"Okay, this is just nasty," I said.

"Hello!"

"Okay," I repeated. "I don't know who you *think* you called, but I am not him . . . or her. Do not call me anymore. You are nasty."

"Hold up," she said. "Is this 582- . . .?"

"No," I retorted. "This is 586- . . ."

I will spare you from what followed out of her mouth. I hung up. She didn't call back.

Was that a harsh approach? Maybe, but knowing me, I'm surprised I remained *that calm* with all of the expletives that were flowing from her mouth, almost as if she had the right to speak to me that way. Yet another lesson about the effects of an unbridled tongue, for sure (James 1:26). But the bigger thing is, it wasn't just about how rude she was being but her feeling like she had to 1) call a guy for sex at all, and 2) send her "goodies" via text mail. What kinda crazy was going on?

Oh, the yin and yang of life. I couldn't have found a better way to intro this chapter. Here I am in a bridal store and a girl is begging for sex on my cell phone. On one hand a woman was outside of my dressing room door preparing for sex *inside of God's purpose* and inside my dressing room was a girl who was cussing me out as she was darn near stalking a guy to have sex *outside of it!*

And you know what? I can only be so upset with that young and apparently very broken woman. I've been where she's been: so caught up in the physical gratification of sexual activity that I don't understand the holistic detriment that sex outside of God's covering brings into my "human trinity"—my mind, body, and spirit.

Not too long ago I watched a movie on Lifetime about women and sexual addiction. (I don't know why Lifetime is called "Television for Women" when most of the characters in their films appear to be, uh, *psycho*.) Surprisingly, this movie was actually pretty good. When the main character finally went in for treatment after sleeping with hundreds of men, her counselor told her that sexual addiction was a form of self-loathing. According to the therapist, sex addicts hate doing it—the kind of sex that includes random partners for random reasons, not the sex act itself. And because of how doing it makes them feel, even if it is just a temporary fix, it helps them escape the guilt and self-condemnation. And the cycle continues.

> *Sexual addiction was a form of self-loathing.*

You're not an addict, right? You can count the number of partners you've had on less than two hands. All of the guys you've been with had the title of boyfriend. Shoot, you may even be a virgin who doesn't do *that* . . . just the other stuff. Yeah, I hear you, and all I have to say to that is, if you are engaging in sex, any kind of sex, outside of God's will for your life, I wouldn't be so sure about labeling yourself a *virgin*.

I recall a famous television therapist saying that an "addiction" is anything that takes us away from our normal way of life. John 10:10 says that Christ came so that we could live life in abundance. Romans 6:23 tells us that the wages of sin is death. First Corinthians 6:9–10 assures us that the unrighteous will not inherit the kingdom of heaven. Do you know who's included on that "righteous-less" list? Fornicators, adulterers, and homosexuals (v. 10). Are you willing to risk an abundant life on earth and eternal life in heaven just to "get some"? If the answer is yes—and it's not just your words but your actions on this earth that will determine that—*then an addict is exactly what you are*. You are willing to risk your eternal life for a quick fix.

Unfortunately, so many of us are using sex to . . . well, let's stop right there for just a moment because that is a message in itself. So many of us are *using* sex. We are not (just) *enjoying* sex, we're using it to make us feel good about ourselves. We are using it as a distraction from the inner and external issues in our daily life. We are using it to get or "keep" a man (heads-up: sex will not keep a man. I've tried numerous times!). But that's just it. In God's perfect design, sex was never meant to be used in an abusive sense. It is to be embraced, celebrated, shared between two committed, covenant partners. A husband and a wife.

When we do what we want, when we want, without going to God about *why* he wanted us to do or not do something, we find ourselves in a compromised state at best, and at worst, a very dangerous one. The reason sex exists is to bring a husband and wife together as one mind, one body, and one spirit.

The second purpose of sex is to replenish the Earth through this act (Gen. 1:28). And because it was an instruction given to mankind in the Garden, I will go one step further by saying that the third purpose of sex—which, when you really think about it is probably the first—is to honor and worship God. God told us how we should have sex, and any time that we follow his instruction, it is an act of obedience to him. First Samuel 15:22 tells us that it is better to obey than to sacrifice.

Have sex within covenant? You are being obedient.

Have sex outside of it? Yes, one way or another, you will have to pay a sacrifice.

That may not be a popular message (see Amos 5:10 Message), but to have sex *any way outside of God's biblical design* is counterfeit. It may seem like the real thing, but it is not. A good lie seems like truth (John 8:44). It is not. If you are partaking in sex outside of marriage (Heb. 13:4; 1 Cor. 6:9), then I encourage you, from personal experience, to spend some real time focusing on the *purpose* behind why God created sex. Covenant and procreation are gifts. The Enemy seeks to steal, kill, and destroy (John 10:10) anything from the Lord in any way that he can.

> *Spend some real time focusing on the* purpos*e behind why God created sex.*

Holy Ground

So, what happened?

That is a miniseries by itself. I will, however, take this moment to plug a book that has helped to keep me abstinent as I ponder the answers to this kind of question. The author is Tim Alan Gardner and the book is *Sacred Sex*. It's written for married people, but as a currently single woman with a high libido, trust me, it's a lifesaver to anyone even semi-struggling on the road to sexual purity (and if you have this book in hand, whether you realize it or not, that would be you!). Two major points about *Sacred Sex* have stayed with me, even in my weakest of moments.

The first is that sex is about oneness more than it is about orgasms. That would make sense, considering the instruction in the Garden of Eden was that a man was to leave his mother and father, be united with his wife, and become *one flesh* (Gen. 2:24). The Bible says the man and his wife were naked and not ashamed (v. 25), giving us license to believe that sexual intercourse took place between them. (I'll get to Tim's second point that I cling to in a few paragraphs.)

Interesting, isn't it, that Scripture doesn't say they were naked and had *an orgasm*? It says they were naked and became one flesh. To be "one" is to be "existing, acting, or considered as a single unit, entity, or individual"; to be "of the same or having a single kind, nature, or condition." The physical act of sexual intercourse brings oneness to two people, two people who desire to be one in their total state of being and have been blessed by God in marriage to be one until death parts them (Matt. 19:6; 22:30).

Okay, please allow me to interject something here as well. One of my eighty million gigs consists of my being a teen mom coordinator for a local nonprofit. Four days a week, I see what sex outside of covenant has done, not just in the lives of the young women I mentor, but in their parents, their children, their friends, the economy, and society as a whole. When I meet with them, one of the main things I ask these teen mothers (who range from thirteen to eighteen) is how they feel about their baby's daddy. Eighty percent of them, and I'm being generous, usually say they can't stand him.

"So why did you have a baby with him?"

"Ms. Shelliiiiie," they whine. "I didn't plaaaaaan on getting pregnant. It just kinda happened."

Nothing "just kinda happens." But what I want us to see is that if he's not "good enough" to be the father of our child, he's not good enough to have sex with us either. Oh, how sad it is that we have come to a place where many women, old and young alike, don't value their body as good enough, a sacred place, holy ground, even though the Bible clearly tells us we are:

> Flee sexual immorality. Every sin that a man does is outside the body, but he who commits sexual immorality sins against his own body. *Or do you not know that your body is the temple of the Holy Spirit who is in you, whom you have from God, and you are not your own? For you were bought*

at a price; therefore glorify God in your body and in your spirit, which are God's.

1 Corinthians 6:18–20 NKJV

Several months ago I went on a fast. An adult, virgin, female friend of mine joined me. During the fast she found herself frustrated because so many of us were finding nuggets of truth in God's Word and beyond, and she wasn't. At the end of the fast, I emailed her to inquire if anything had struck her during the time of discipline. Her response was truly classic: "Well, I did get one thing: stop screwing the Holy Spirit."

That may sound crude, but let me tell you what she meant. This was her way of saying masturbation is not the way to go. It's not, and we'll get to that in the next chapter. I'm bringing it up now, though, because I want to make it clear that *any kind of sexual immorality* is like "screwing" the Holy Spirit. According to the Word of God, the Holy Spirit, our helper, our comforter, our conscience, dwells within us—we are his temple, literally. Some of the more traditional folks may feel uncomfortable with masturbation being addressed in this way, but personally, I think one of the biggest problems with the topic of sexual immorality is that either we try to ignore it or speak about it in a way that doesn't make it sound as horrifically degrading as it really is. I am not stretching biblical truth by cosigning on my friend's resolve.

Paul clearly wrote that our bodies are the temple of the Holy Spirit, and we were bought with a price; we are not our own. In other words, we shouldn't be doing whatever we feel like doing with our bodies, because we are vessels that belong to God. The price that was paid for us was the shedding of Christ's blood. Whenever we have sex outside of covenant, it's basically like spitting on the sacrifice. *So what, you died so that I could be redeemed? I want what I want,* we may think, *and I'm going to get it, even if it hurts you, even if it's like nailing you to the cross all over again.*

Yes. When you have sex outside of the way God created, *that is exactly what you are saying to him*—that what he did for you and what he thinks of you don't matter and neither do you or your body. Listen, you *do* matter, and sexually, you matter so much God said that you deserve a husband, not just a sex partner.

My mind-set started to change when I stopped looking at the *benefits* of sex and started looking more into the *purpose* of it. *Purpose* can be defined as the reason for which something exists or is done, made, used, and so on, an intended or desired result, end, aim, goal, practical result, effect, or advantage.

We are vessels that belong to God.

The last time you had sex, any kind of sex (which we will deal with in chapter 3, but yes, that would include oral sex and mutual or self-masturbation), did you take a moment and ask what purpose it was serving? If you're like me, I'm sure a part of the "purpose" was to get the physical benefits, but please understand that the *perks of sex* are never meant to replace the *purpose of sex*. Not in God's view, anyway, and at the end of the day (every day), it's his view that matters most (see Mark 12:30).

Now to the second point that continues to resonate in my head from Tim Alan Gardner's *Sacred Sex* book. It's actually a quote that he pulled from M. Scott Peck's book *Further Along the Road Less Traveled*: "Sex is the closest that many people will ever come to a spiritual experience. Indeed, it is because it is a spiritual experience of sorts that so many chase after it with a repetitive, desperate kind of abandon. Often, whether they realize it or not, they are searching for God."[1]

According to Peck's insight, sex is a spiritual experience and many people use sex as a path to God. Does that make you feel "icky" inside? If so, you need more sexual reprogramming than you might think because Mr. Peck is dead-on. Do you think the Enemy would put so much energy into something if it wasn't a grand spiritual experience? After all, he is a spirit; he understands the strength of the spirit world in a way that we, being both flesh and spirit, do not (see Gal. 5:16–17). And because of this fact, just as he did in the Garden, the Enemy tries to twist the blessing of sex to present it in a way that will ultimately curse us.

I'll give you an example.

Homosexuality

A couple of people in my life have chosen the homosexual lifestyle. Scripture, both the Old and New Testament (as if that should matter), is clear about what God thinks of it (see Romans 1, for starters). What I tell my friends is that if they do not reverence the Bible as the guideline for their lives, then I totally get it (as much as I can). But the Bible is not Piccadilly's. It's not some cafeteria where you can decide what you want to keep and what you want to throw away based on your personal preferences. To come to the conclusion that, as a Christian, you know better than God what's best for you is, to me, the ultimate act of sacrilege. But when my homosexual friends want to get into a discussion about whether it's right or wrong, purpose is what usually comes to my mind and out of my mouth:

"OK, let's say that you do love your partner. Do you want to have children?"

Most of them say yes.

"So, outside of adopting, how are you going to do that without breaking covenant?"

Crickets.

"And if you do go the in vitro route, why is that? Heterosexuals do it because they try to get pregnant and can't. But you don't even have the hope of getting pregnant naturally."

More crickets.

To me, this is a good example of what happens when sex is outside of purpose. One purpose of sex is for two bodies to become one flesh—to be naked and not ashamed. I have watched lesbianism influence many young women I work with, and one of the things we talk about is how our bodies were made with everything we need. Is it just me, or does homosexual need a *lot* of extra assistance for it to work? I mean, if I were to go on a desert island today with a guy— umm, I mean, my husband—all we need is each other. No "extra stuff" is required. That alone should be a cue. Ecclesiastes 3:14 tells us that what God does, he does forever, and *nothing* can be added to or taken from it. In God's design for sex, dildos and strap-ons are not needed. People's body parts are not torn and abused. You get my point. In God's purpose for things, there is no need for substitution—there is no lack. But there is another purpose for sex as well:

> Then God blessed them, and God said to them, "Be fruitful and multiply; fill the earth and subdue it; have dominion over the fish of the sea, over the birds of the air, and over every living thing that moves on the earth."

> Genesis 1:28 NKJV

And here is where my friends seem to become the most stumped. In Genesis 1:26–27, God said he made man—male and female—in his image. I'm sure this had the Enemy ticked off. It wasn't just about us being created. It was about us being created to be a replica of God on earth. And so, when God created a way for man and woman to make more like him, the Enemy came up with a counterfeit plan. I don't doubt my homosexual friends love their partners, and you will never see me jumping on a bandwagon to support abusing them just because they don't agree with the theology I model my life after. But I will say this, and unapologetically so: "If all of us were homosexual, who's left to procreate?" In essence, wouldn't the Enemy's mission of "stealing, killing, and destroying" human life (John 10:10) be ultimately accomplished? Sometimes we are so focused on trying to get what we want, we don't realize what we put ourselves at the potential risk of losing by obtaining it.

Now, before the "bashers" jump in with a "Hooray!" the other side of this is that I am not one of those people who thinks what homosexuals do is worse than other sins. Look, I had heterosexual sex outside of covenant and chose to allow four of my own children to die because of it. God is not pleased with that—at all. But my point in bringing all of this up is that when we do what we want, when we want, without going to God about *why* he wanted us to do or not do something, we find ourselves in a compromised state and sometimes a very dangerous one.

The reason sex exists is to bring a man and his wife together as one—mind, body, and spirit. The second purpose of sex is to replenish the earth through this act. And, because it was an instruction given to humankind in the garden, I will go one step further by saying the third purpose of sex (which when you think about it is probably the first) is to honor and worship God. God told us how we should have sex, and any time we follow his instruction, it is an act of obedience to him. First Samuel 15:22 tells us that it is better to obey than to sacrifice. Have sex within covenant? You are being obedient. Have sex outside of it? Yes, one way or another, you will have to pay a price.

If you are single, think about the last sexual relationship you were in. How much did you gain and how much did you lose? Sex inside of purpose, based on the definition, is to be a supernaturally advantageous experience for both the husband and the wife. Sex outside of purpose . . . well, I don't know about you, but over the course of time I lost a lot more than those few hours that a couple nights a week ever gave me— not because the sex didn't feel good, but because I know God has more in mind for my sex life than physical pleasure. He

God has more in mind for my sex life than physical pleasure.

wants my soul to have peace; he wants my emotions to be tended to; he wants my mind at rest; he wants a "till death do us part" covenant in place. He wants me to have sex, with a purpose. According to the Word of God, only a God-ordained, biblically defined marriage can provide that.

God's Sexual Ideal

If you are single, think about the last sexual relationship you were in. How much did you gain and how much did you lose? Sex inside of God's purpose, based on the definition, is to be a supernaturally advantageous experience for both the husband and the wife.

When it comes to sex outside of God's purpose, well, I don't know about you, but over the course of time, I lost a lot more than those few hours a couple of nights a week ever gave me—not because sex didn't feel good, but because when I was born on June 17, 1974, I know God had more in mind for my sex life than physical pleasure. He wanted my soul to have peace . . . he wanted my emotions to be tended to . . . he wanted my mind to be at rest . . . he wanted a "till death do us part" covenant in place. He wanted me to have sex with a purpose. According to the Word of God, only a God-ordained, biblically defined marriage can provide that.

But you and your "boo" love each other, right? You've been together for years and sex hasn't changed the relationship. If that is your argument, you are in more trouble than I thought. To believe that life is a game of Monopoly and that, when it comes to God's law, you are somehow the only one to get a "Get Out of Jail Free" pass is to have your mind in the greatest state of deceit. God is no respecter of persons (Rom. 2:11), and James 1:22–24 admonishes us to: "Do what God's teaching says; when you only listen and do nothing, you are fooling yourselves. Those who hear God's teaching and do nothing are like people who look at themselves in a mirror. They see their faces and then go away and quickly forget what they looked like."

Again, while I hope this book will help to convert some nonbelievers, I know that the main focus of it is to convict those who claim to be disciples of Christ already. Well, according to the Bible, the only way you can be considered his disciple is if you abide in the Word of God, and the Word of God says that we are to wait until marriage to have sex—no ifs, ands, or buts about it:

> Live a life of love just as Christ loved us and gave himself for us as a sweet-smelling offering and sacrifice to God. *But there must be no sexual sin among you*, or any kind of evil or greed. Those things are not right for God's holy people. Also, there must be no evil talk among you, and you must not speak foolishly or tell evil jokes. These things are not right for you. Instead, you should be giving thanks to God.
>
> Ephesians 5:2–4

Currently on Facebook, I am doing something called a "Wife Curriculum Class." One day a wife signed on and read something I was sharing about abstinence. She paid me one of the nicest compliments I have received in quite some time: "I love how you are taking sex back and putting it where it belongs."

I knew what she meant. It amazes me how we have come to a place where we are letting the way the world has sex set the tone for us believers. Up until chapter 9, that is pretty much what we will be discussing. Sex doesn't belong to the world. Sex belongs to those who love God and reverence his order, his way of doing things. If you are bold enough to sit through the next several chapters, while at times it is pretty "Wow! Did she just say that?" please know that my desire is not to shock anyone or disrespect anything of God. However, I am a firm believer that since the Enemy has gotten so bold in his tactics and since he can't do anything to me without God's permission (Job 1:9–12), I need to be even bolder.

One of the greatest lies I used to fall for was that I would never be fully free from the sexual ties that had me bound. I don't want you falling for that same lie. Okeydokey?

Sex has a purpose and it's time we found it. Right here and now—no matter how raw, candid, or revealing it may be.

Godly Livin'

- - - - - - - - - - -

You lie down with dogs, you get up with fleas and wonder
    why you're itchin' for lovin'
Thought you could bring a man to his knees with your body
    rather than prayin'
And now you're caught up in quite a mess, your plan seems
    to be quickly fadin'
It was problems you created while it was love that you thought
    you were makin'
So, now you want an easy way out, tryin' to get tight with
    God after being so loose
Perpetrating in church as if you're living right and like you're
    a woman of virtue
My Darling, that's a process and not a goal, it takes more
    than a conscious decision
You wanna turn your life around, get out of lust's bed and get
    into Godly livin'

© Shellie R. Warren, 1999

Sexual Additives, Part One

Closet Activities

But there must be no sexual sin among you, or any kind of evil or greed. Those things are not right for God's holy people.

Ephesians 5:3

I used to think masturbation was not really sex because it only involved me. That's a very limited view of human sexuality, and it isn't going to work for women.

Betty Dodson, intimacy advice columnist

Heads-up, people: If you thought the last chapter was a ride, you may want to brace yourself for this one. We are about to hit some "closet sexual activities" head-on. We are about to see 'em and call 'em for what they really are. And prayerfully, by the time we are done, some of you will no longer have the delusional attitude I used to have when I first stopped having intercourse while doing some of this, uh, other stuff.

Have you ever found yourself saying, "Well, at least I'm not having *sex*," or "At least I am not putting myself at the risk of being humiliated by having my business put out there," or "At least I'm not a ho like so-and-so." Uh, what made you come to that conclusion? Because the things you were doing weren't on the "naughty" list? Hmph.

Is anyone familiar with Karrine Steffans? She is the author of the *New York Times* bestseller *Video Vixen*. Before being known as a writer, Karrine earned a reputation not for the *sexual intercourse* she was having but the *oral sex* she was giving.

I remember when I first asked my mother about oral sex. I was in high school, and unlike a lot of "church moms," she gave a really healthy response: "That is a very intimate act and it should be reserved for a very intimate relationship." That is all I *remember* her saying on the issue, but you can believe that with all of the books and videos on waiting until marriage she had me read when I was growing up, she fully believed that "intimate" was synonymous with marriage, and I wish I had taken heed to her wisdom.

When God created us, when he encouraged us not to cast our pearls before swine (Matt. 7:6), he had a reason for saying it. I don't know if you realize it or not, but there is more to "swine" than pigs. *Swine* can be defined as a coarse, gross, or brutishly sensual person.

As if that were not revelatory enough, let me say that "pearl" is not some random metaphor either. It does not represent just one body part. Our *entire body* should be reverenced as a jewel, a gem, the ultimate gift from God to our spouse, the kind of thing a man should spend all that he has, including his single life, to get. (If you've never read the parable of the pearl, you can check it out in Matthew 13:45–46.)

When I started on this abstinence journey—rather reluctantly, I might add—I'm going to be honest with you: my plan was to go without *penetration* for as long as I could. I had been into "additives" for so long that I initially told myself there was *no way* I could go without masturbation on a regular basis (two to three times per week to replace the sex that I was used to having at least once a week), and to get even more real, oral sex was going to have to come around, shoot, at least for the holiday season (and that included all of the ones that my government-working and Jewish friends observed!). God was just going to have to understand that, while I would "lay off" sexual intercourse from my life (temporarily), I had no intention of giving up my "side gigs."

You know what? I wouldn't have believed it if you told me, but since making the pledge on January 9, 2007, to really take this "without sex thing" seriously—meaning, since I really made a personal commitment to not engage in sex, of any form, again until marriage—not so much as a kiss has been added to my sexual performance résumé. Again, that wasn't the plan, but the more I started understanding and valuing the purpose of sex and the purpose of me (chapter 8), the more I didn't think a man had the right to any of my temple. When God created me and saw that I was *good*, that meant all of me: head to toe, mouth and midsection, on the giving and receiving end of physical intimacy and affection. And when God created the purpose for sex, he wanted me to respect it. Oral sex is sex and if you're going to have it (there's no Scripture that says you can't; that's solely up to you and your husband), you need to have it with your spouse as one-half of a married couple. Masturbation? You don't need to be having that at all, but I will get to this in a moment.

Even as I am on this road of sexual restoration, and even though I haven't even kissed anyone (yet) since January 9, 2007, let me say this: I am not the Joshua Harris *I Kissed*

> *Our* entire body *should be reverenced as a jewel.*

Dating Goodbye kind of girl, although I do have respect for anyone doing what he or she needs to do to be what God wants that person to be. And in this case, it is to be sexually whole. It would appear that no kissing, and courting, not dating, worked for Joshua and his wife, and God bless them. However, just because that was how they did it and it's what I'm doing, I am not implying that kissing or dating outside of marriage is wrong (somebody find me a Scripture to support otherwise) nor am I trying to push the rigidness of what I'm doing onto you. But I will say that having crossed all kinds of sexual lines, I now liken a lot of sexual activity, including intimate kissing, to eating a cracker while fasting: sometimes, when you're starving, "eating a li'l something" does nothing but make you all the more upset. Honestly, I'm too old (and wise) to be starting something and stopping it all of the time. Kiss me intimately but keep your hands at your sides? Why does that just seem like it would add to the stress of abstinence and not relieve it? But again, that's just me.

Flesh-Satisfaction Substitutes

A friend of mine by the name of Brian Watts once preached that one of the biggest problems in the church is that there is a difference between preference, conviction, and commandments, and we are preaching way too many preferences and not enough commandments. "Thou shalt not kiss" is not a commandment, at least that I've seen, in the Word of God, and so I'm not going to preach against it like it is one. But when it comes to some of these other acts, well, I am about to show you how, in doing them, you are breaking, at the very least, the seventh commandment: "Thou shalt not commit adultery" (Exod. 20:14 KJV)—because any man who is not your husband either is or probably will be someone's husband. And at the very most, in addition to that commandment, you are breaking "Thou shalt have no other gods before me" (v. 3 KJV), "Thou shalt not steal" (v. 15 KJV), "Thou shalt not bear false witness against thy neighbor" (which the New Century and Message versions define as "lying," and I would say that includes lying to yourself!), and "Thou shalt not covet" (want what someone else has—v. 17 KJV). I can understand why James 2:10 tells us that if we have stumbled in any point of the law, we are guilty of breaking it all!

That said, you might be curious about why I titled this chapter "Sexual Additives." A couple of years ago I hired a trainer who told me I needed to alter my diet. I *love* sugar and so I started reading up on sugar substitutes—something that would taste like what I wanted but wouldn't have the same consequences. I began using a lot of different substitutes. But life experience has taught me that just because I *can* doesn't necessarily mean that I *should*.

We are preaching way too many preferences and not enough commandments.

While I don't want to name any sugar substitutes, let's just say there was a certain pastel-colored packet I grew to be particularly fond of—several times a day, especially in my sweet tea. One day, one of my super–health conscious friends looked at me as I was pouring a packet into my drink and gasped, "Did you know that *saccharin* is in there and that it's really bad for you?" I knew the apparent health concern with such a sugar substitute at the time, but because of how it tasted, I didn't too much care. To me, it was doing just what it was created to do: satisfy my desire for sugar without packing on the calories. It was doing something else to me as well, something that my friend made sure I knew. I will not pretend to be a health professional, but after doing some saccharin research, here's a superbrief tutorial:

• It's a man-made sweetener.

- It's three hundred times sweeter than natural sugar.
- In large doses, it could lead to cancer.

That sweet stuff comes with high risks. Sure, it's a different kind of risk than natural sugar, but it's risky nonetheless. When it comes to sexual additives—things that are not sexual intercourse themselves but are used as flesh-satisfaction substitutes—there should be a spiritual warning label put on them. I'd venture to say the warning for sexual additives would read something like this:

- Man-made
- Can be three hundred times more addictive than sexual intercourse
- In large doses, can seriously impair your sex life

Now for the people skimming through this book in a bookstore while trying to decide if you should buy it, the bottom line of this chapter is: *God-ordained sex was made for a married man and woman.* Not a man and a man, not a woman and a woman, not a man with two women (or two men and a woman), *and* not you and yourself. Again, because we now know the *purpose* of sex, we understand that it's about bringing oneness to a husband and wife. When it comes to oral sex, the word *sex* is a clue that it is wrong to engage in outside of marriage. When it comes to masturbation, because it is about self-stimulation and you don't need to become "one" with someone whom you should already be "one" with, then yes, to do it at all (in or out of marriage) is wrong. And I mean, *wrong*, as defined "not in accordance with what is morally right or good; deviating from truth or fact; erroneous; not correct in action, judgment, opinion, method, etc., as a person; in error; not proper or usual; not in accordance with requirements or recommended practice; out of order; awry; amiss; not suitable or appropriate."

Discern, Don't Experience

For those of you who actually purchased this book (thank you) and are looking for more detailed information as to why you might need it at this time in your life, let's get to it.

While I was growing up, there was a Bible teacher in my Christian-based high school who played a really significant role in changing the way I looked at life, especially when it came to moving away from man's obsession with religion and delving into the importance of having a relationship with God. If you are out there, Chuck Stanford, I adore you.

When it came to the issue of sex, I remember him telling my senior class that one of the problems with doing "everything but" was that, psychologically, if we were not careful, we could find ourselves staying in that place, even in marriage. After a while our bodies would shut down after a certain point because that is what we taught it to do, *because we trained it to be that way* before proper covenant marriage status. See how powerful the mind is?

That seed was definitely planted in my mind, but like most kids when they hear an adult tell them something they don't want to hear, I didn't really nurture it. I put myself in a position where I had to learn the hard way. My mother often says, "Discernment prevents experience from being your teacher." When it comes to this chapter's subject, no greater words have been spoken.

In high school I let a couple of guys fondle me and when I met my first boyfriend in college, I really liked him, so there was a constant war between the "good girl" and the girl who didn't want to be so good (Gal. 5:16–17). And so, since all I could remember was "Don't have sexual intercourse" and "Naughty girls get pregnant," I came up with things to tell myself to avoid those sentences playing over and over in my head while I was making out with my boyfriend: *Touching my breasts isn't having sex and it can't get me pregnant. Grinding, or dry humping* (as the "over-30s folks" call it) *isn't having sex and it can't get me pregnant. Even letting him, you know . . . touch the place where if-he-doesn't-keep-his-clothes-on-could-get-me-pregnant . . . isn't having sex and won't get me pregnant.*

Initially, it seemed like a win-win. But for whom?

Okay, you may not have seen this curveball coming, but do you know one of the biggest problems with the "everything but" syndrome? I liken it to sneaking a peak at a present on Christmas Eve instead of Christmas Day. It's not time to play with it the way you want, but at the same time you already know what it is and so a lot of the thrill is gone by the time it's yours for the taking. That alone should be reason for pause.

Another part of the problem with you-can-do-everything-but-enter-in is that it teaches you to become a very selfish sex partner. Doing everything but sexual intercourse is really about coming up with a way to get the physical benefits of sex without having to deal with all of the physical responsibilities, right? Well, the truth (see John 8:32) is, when you have sex with your partner, it's not just about what *you* can get from *him*. First Corinthians 7:4 tells us the husband has authority over the wife's body and the wife has authority over the husband's.

Sex is meant to be a mutually gratifying experience. Ladies, when you let guys do everything other than penetrate, you are not putting their needs at the top of your list (and you know this by how frustrated they usually are when they leave your house). What you have done is found a way to rationalize your craving to get what you want without giving it (all) up. That's a form of manipulation. And using what you've got to get what you want is not of God.

First Corinthians 7:34 says that an unmarried person cares for the things of the Lord, *"that she may be holy both in body and in spirit."* To be "holy" is to be "specially recognized as or declared sacred by religious use or authority, consecrated" and to have "a spiritually pure quality." Please tell me how you are doing that while letting a guy rub all over your body? On top of that, how are you pleasing the Lord by sending one of his personal image-bearing creations home frustrated, while most likely, on his way home (or to some other gal's house) he commits another act (that I am about to get to in a second) to relieve his frustration?

When it comes to sex, neither party should ever leave the experience feeling used or discontent. Having any kind of sex outside of marriage, because God's covering is not present, is going to do just that in some shape, form, or fashion. And not one time, not ten times, but every single time. When you fail to complete the sexual act, someone is going to walk away with his or her mind, spirit, or body (if not all three) totally lacking peace. That is not the way God intended sex to be. When it comes to "everything but," at the end of the day, that also means everything but complete and total satisfaction.

Sex is meant to be a mutually gratifying experience.

Oral Sex

Two other things need to be addressed in this chapter as well. I'll go with oral sex next.

First of all, if one more person tells me that it's not really sex, I'm going to scream! If you are one of those people, just listen to what you are saying: oral *sex* is not really *sex*. I mean, read that again. "Sex" is right there in the phrase. *It is sex.* And while I understand, from a physical standpoint, that it is pleasurable, what I don't understand is how people can think it puts them any less at risk. Sure, the act can't get you pregnant, but it can actually do a whole lot worse. According to the American Medical Health Association, one in five people in the US have an STD, with HPV and chlamydia being the most commonly contracted. Less than half of adults eighteen to forty-four have been tested for an STD (other than HIV/AIDS), and two-thirds of hepatitis B infections are transmitted sexually. My point? According to the Centers for Disease Control and Prevention, in 2002, more than 90 percent of males and 88 percent of females ages twenty-five to forty-four reported having oral sex with an opposite-sex partner.[1] That means that more than a few of you have been, pardon the pun, not using your head wisely from a physical and mental perspective. I'll show you why.

Paul O'Malley, a researcher for the San Francisco Health Department, published in the late '90s an insightful and graphic article on oral sex and HIV transmission. Here is an excerpt of his findings:

> Receptive oral sex or "giving a blow job" is considered *more risky* because of the potential that more HIV-infected fluid will enter the body. When someone is giving a blow job, not only is there the potential exposure to semen and precome, there is also the potential exposure to blood from a penile cut, sore, or abrasion, or even from an irritated piercing.
>
> Furthermore, if the man receiving the blow job has another infection in addition to HIV, he may have an unusually high level of HIV present in his body fluids. This is because his immune system may not be as efficient at controlling HIV, since it is also trying to contain the other virus or bacteria. An added problem is that if the additional infection is localized in the penis, then there will probably be urethra inflammation. If so, his penile fluids may contain high levels of "infection-fighting" white blood cells, which unfortunately also contain HIV. All this could amount to increased infectiousness.[2]

When it comes to oral sex, sure, you won't get *pregnant*, but you can definitely put yourself in the position of seriously impairing, if not totally destroying, your life—and that's just physically.

Now, if you are a married person reading this, please don't take this out of context. I have no business telling *you* what to do in *your* bedroom. Of all the things that I have been, a sexual voyeur is not one of them; however, I will say that with this kind of information available to the masses, I'm not sure why anyone would want to do such a risky act *outside of covenant*. Women like Karrine Steffans and many others (check out rap artist the Game's song "Wouldn't Get Far") have shown what it will do to your reputation, and medical reports reflect what it could do to damage the one and only body temple you will get in this lifetime.

Thing is, a lot of people think oral sex is a way of avoiding the physical consequences of sexual intercourse, but that's a myth that I will attempt to prove false right here and now: one of my ex-boyfriends got an STD from receiving oral sex (that's right: *receiving it!*). The Word says we are like a vapor (James 4:14). With life being so fleeting and fragile, it seems to me you would want to avoid not only the activities that would create life out of season but the ones that could end it out of season as well. Oral sex, like sex, is reserved for those who can have sex. If you're not married, that's not you.

Masturbation

Masturbation—the ultimate form of single sex. Woody Allen was once quoted as saying, "Don't knock masturbation. It's sex with someone I love." Ha-ha. Funny man. I can definitely see where he's coming from because I used to "love on myself" pretty often, but I'll tell you what: at the end of the day, I've had a Snickers bar that's satisfied me more and I don't even like Snickers all that much!

Masturbation doesn't come close to the kind of sexual experience that takes place when you have sex with someone else. So how and why did I get caught up in it? This is where I want to remind you of just how powerful words are; indeed death and life are in the power of the tongue just as King Solomon said (Prov. 18:21). Even with all that I had experienced sexually, partially due to sexual abuse and partially due to sexual misuse, it wasn't until my second year of college that I really entertained the lifestyle of masturbation (and trust me, for many people, it is just that—a lifestyle).

One day, while having dinner, a college professor came and sat at the table that I was sharing with some friends. He was always one of our favorites and so he was able to play and joke around with us more than most. However, in hindsight, I realize that what he was really doing was verbally molesting us. When our professor asked us about our sex lives, I didn't think anything about it. But now? Why in the heck was a man, who was older then than I am now, asking us about whether we were having sex and if we were having orgasms? I mean, really?

But as he went into his psychobabble about how you can only teach a man to please you after you know how to please yourself, it got me thinking. I was having sex, but I wasn't having that crawl-up-the-walls kind of sex that my college suite mates were talking about. And so, after reading a few articles on the subject of masturbation, I tried it. The first time, like the first time I had sex, it was awkward and strange. There was nothing really *pleasurable* about it. But I got sick of not "having my eyes opened" through sexual climaxes, and since I was too afraid to tell my boyfriend that I wasn't enjoying it in the way he seemed to be, I figured I would put my energies into myself. I would be patient with me for as long as it took.

It didn't take long.

If you have never masturbated, please listen to me: DON'T. It's a junkie fix like no other, and it took many, many years for me to overcome it. Honestly, I still battle with not doing it when I get the random urge. Sometimes, especially when I am ovulating (a time when most women are the most, umm, amorous), I still want to sneak a moment or two for myself.

I used to think, *It may not be steak (full-on sex), more like a hamburger, but it's still beef, right?*

A lot of sweat and tears have brought me to the conclusion that masturbation, a.k.a. sex with yourself, is no better than "everything but" or oral sex. I've said it before, and I'm sure I'll say it a billion more times before I die, but sex is not created for anyone other than a husband and his wife, period. It's a little odd explaining the pitfalls of masturbation in this way, but bear with me. Because I didn't have my first orgasm from intercourse (technically it was from oral sex, but most consistently from masturbation), over time I started relying on what gave me the most pleasure—not sex or oral sex but masturbation. I had sex (usually including oral sex) mostly for the guy and to keep a hold of the relationship for as long as I could, and saved masturbation just for me.

Now, let me stop here for a sec. I definitely liked the affection and attention that came with having sex. I love being kissed and held and some of the other stuff. I know this doesn't translate perfectly to married women (or maybe it does), but as a single gal having sex outside of covenant, the peak for the man was oftentimes my valley. While we were lying there, there were definitely moments when I was thinking, *I can't wait until he leaves so that I can finally . . .*

And therein lies a huge part of the problem. It bears repeating, probably a few times in the course of this book, that 1 Corinthians 7:4 tells us that the man does not have authority over his body; the wife does. And vice versa. Masturbation was setting me up for the habit of having authority over my own body, even in marriage, to be the master of my own pleasure, to take me away from the purpose *and* pleasures of sex. In healthy marital sex, I open myself up to love and trust my husband enough for us to learn *together* how I can be pleased. Sex is not about one person being happy. Sex is about two people making one another happy.

Mutual Masturbation

I remember having a conversation/semi-argument with a husband and wife who are, let's just say, very "free" with their bodies, even around their children. They were talking to me about how their daughter sees them while they are getting dressed and how she is starting to ask questions about her father, umm, not having what she has. Personally, I think when children start asking, it's time for them to stop seeing, because I believe that a girl's first view of "what she doesn't have" should be her husband's. That may sound ideal and unrealistic, but as someone who will not have that testimony upon entering her marriage, I believe it will make life a lot easier for the little princesses-in-training to take that route. Sex isn't about appealing to only one of your senses. Seeing is just as much a vital part of the experience as hearing or touching. *You shouldn't see what doesn't belong to you until it belongs to you.* Vows before God are what make that happen.

Although mutual masturbation is not an act that I really took part in while I was sexually active, I have many friends who do. It's unfortunate that sexual purity has not been taught to many of us in a way where we don't see that there is more to sexual intimacy between a man and his wife than engaging in intercourse. To see one another naked? That is intimate. To touch one another in intimate ways? That is sacred. Hebrews 13:4 tells us that the marriage bed is undefiled. A pure bed is one where a husband and wife can enjoy nakedness and the joys of one another, even besides intercourse. For you and your partner to either stimulate one another to the point of orgasm or to watch one another do it to oneself, that is what would be considered "mutual masturbation."

Whenever I speak to young people about sex, one of the first things I ask is, "What's the purpose of sex?" The answer I often get is "orgasms." An orgasm is indeed a *benefit* of sex, but not the *purpose*—the reason for which it was created. Mutual masturbation may be a way to avoid a pregnancy (perhaps), but not the consequences of lust and impurity. And, even if you're doing it as a virgin, your body is not the only part of you that is involved in the sexual act. The memories of partaking in those kinds of acts with men you are not married to, trust me, can end up haunting you for years to come.

Mutual masturbation was never my "drug of choice," but because I've had multiple sex partners, you have no idea how many times I have "seen" other men in my mind other than the guy I was dating at the time. And not just men I have been sexually active with, but penises I have seen in porn (we'll talk about *that* in the next chapter) or even while going to the movies with friends (some movies don't even give you a rating warning—*The Reader* is one example that immediately comes to mind). Access to that kind of information can really mess with your mind, because then you find yourself making comparisons that should never be made.

An orgasm is a **benefit** *of sex, but not the* **purpose.**

One of the reasons it took so long for me to shake my first love was because he was my introduction to all things sexual. To me, everything about him was the greatest because I didn't really have all that much else to go on; there wasn't much to compare him with. *And that's just how God wanted it to be*—only he wanted it to be with my husband and not my boyfriend.

Because I didn't want this book to be all about me, although a lot of it will be about me (hope you don't mind), I interviewed some wives who had sex outside of covenant to get their insights on the consequences that came just so you can see that I am not the exception to the rule. For many women, even when they married the person they fornicated with, there are many mountains to overcome. (BTW, the names have been changed so they can stay happily married.)

Karen, late 20s, married for five years: "One of the biggest problems with having sex before marriage is that you have sex on your terms. Everything about my single sex life seemed great because my boyfriend and I were all about making great impressions. He wanted to make sure that I enjoyed sex because it was a part of the way he was pursuing me. However, after we got married, it seemed that he got really lazy with pleasing me—like, since I was his, he didn't need to put as much effort in. That caused me to start masturbating. I still do it to this day. I don't think he knows though."

Amanda, early 30s, married for eight years: "We loved having oral sex while we were dating. It was low-risk behavior to us. But after getting married and especially since living with him and seeing some of his nasty habits, it's not something I do with him nearly as much. I know it bothers him, but there's nothing like seeing a pair of skid marks on some boxers and then your husband coming into the room grinning. Had I not experienced the 'always clean,' 'always romantic,' 'always perfect' side of sex before marriage, I would probably not feel so disgusted with some of the reality of it now."

Lauren, mid 20s, married for three years: "I prefer masturbation. I always have. My husband and I waited until marriage, but even with as hard as he tries to please me, sex is something that I really do for him. Masturbation, I do for me."

When it comes to sex, especially sex within the will of God, there is no substitute. If after reading this chapter you are feeling convicted to stop using other flesh-satisfaction practices, praise God and good for you.

In chapter 7, we will address how to deal with the transition from sexual brokenness to sexual wholeness, but for now, pray for the desire to become a new creation in Christ. When you do that, 2 Corinthians 5:17 tells us that old things will pass away and *all things* will become new. You didn't get into these strongholds overnight and there's a big chance that you won't get out of them overnight as well, but hopefully, your mind-set is changing.

You're further along than you think. Don't let guilt tell you otherwise (see Rom. 8:1).

Girl Addicted

"Being a girl who is addicted to pornography stinks. All I hear about is men (guys) being addicted to it, but never girls. It's like people assume that girls are too innocent to consider looking at pornography, when I know many girls who are addicted to it. First, I feel the guilt from porn in general. Then, I feel ashamed because I'm a girl looking at it. Finally, I start putting myself down and I think, *I'm pathetic.*

"I've tried so many times to stop, but I just can't seem to kill it completely. It's worse when I'm stressed or the family life isn't so great. Then it's like an escape.

"It has definitely changed my relationship with God too. I feel more distant with Him and every time I want to talk to Him I feel guilty. Like I'm such a screw up and how could He still love me. I've heard it my whole life, how you just have to ask for forgiveness and He can wipe your slate clean. But how could He still want to forgive me if I keep saying I won't look at it and then I do that day or a few days later?

"I suppose I'm just venting. It's not like I can talk to my friends about this kind of thing . . . I don't know.

"Anyone have any advice or comments? Thanks for reading."

Laci, an XXXchurch.com blog reader

Sexual Additives, Part Two

Porn . . . in All Forms

The eye is a light for the body. If your eyes are good, your whole body will be full of light. But if your eyes are evil, your whole body will be full of darkness. And if the only light you have is really darkness, then you have the worst darkness.

Matthew 6:22–23

My reaction to porn films is as follows: After the first ten minutes, I want to go home and screw. After the first 20 minutes, I never want to screw again as long as I live.

Erica Jong, award-winning author and poet

I'm not sure if it will come as a surprise to you or not, but the women's blog reader, Laci, whose testimony opens up this chapter is only fourteen. That's right, she's a teenager, a young, female teenager who is currently addicted to porn. One of the reasons a lot of these chapters open up with testimonies like this one is because I want you to see just how serious sex outside of purpose has become and how many ways it manifests itself.

Do you recall how Rachel described sex with her husband at the beginning of chapter 2? How she said she loved that from day one there was no shame, no memories of boyfriends-past haunting her? And yet look at so many of these other stories. So many people have done it "their way" and have experienced dire and at times horrifically unpredictable consequences as a direct result. I don't know about you, but more and more I am seeing that sex outside of covenant is also sex outside of the proper covering that we all should have: the covering of our self-image, self-worth, and self-protection.

This chapter is going to address the issue of porn addiction candidly as it relates to women. Unfortunately, it's still not talked about, both in and out of the church, as much as it should be. Even in this day and age, porn is seen to be more "a man's problem" or pleasure, depending on whom and when you ask, but I have some stats that may surprise you when it comes to just how much women are being affected by what I consider to be a spiritual stronghold *and* social epidemic.

According to "Top Ten Internet Pornography Statistics" by Jerry Ropelato featured on Internet-Feature-Review.com:

> Every second $3,075.64 is being spent on pornography. Every second 28,258 internet users are viewing pornography. In that same second 372 internet users are typing adult search terms into search engines. Every 39 minutes a new pornographic video is being created in the U.S.[1]

This is sad in itself, but let's look at how it affects women. While it's another book entirely, wives suffer in myriad ways from their husband's porn addiction (check out the "Spouses" blog on XXXchurch.com, and www.PornAddictHubby.com

has some fascinating information on their site as well); however, a startling number of women, married and single, are using porn for their own personal gratification as well.

According to the pornography statistics published on Family SafeMedia.com and provided by Internet-Filter-Review.com, 28 percent of those who admit to having a sexual addiction are women.[2] Brigham Young University's porn study reported that 17 percent of all women struggle with pornography addiction and 13 percent of women admit to accessing pornography at work.[3] As a matter of fact, approximately one in three visitors of all adult websites are women, and 70 percent of women keep their cyberactivities secret.[4]

These must be "worldly" women, you say. I wouldn't be so quick to judge. BYU also reported that 47 percent of Christians said pornography is a major problem in the home.[5] Thirty-four percent of female readers of the *Today's Christian Woman* online newsletter admitted to accessing internet porn in a recent poll, and one out of every six women, including Christians, are struggling with an addiction to pornography.[6]

LightedCandle.org (a nationwide movement dedicated to eradicating pornography) posted that according to Divorce Wizards.com (a website enabling online divorces), "43 percent of American women suffer from Female Sexual Dysfunction" and "More than 15 percent of online-porn pornography addicts develop sexual behavior that disrupts their lives."[7]

This information, without question, is disturbing enough, but it's the following finding that I really think will bring about a sobering acceptance of the reality that porn is not some act that "those people over there do" nor is it a harmless set of fantasies that aren't "as bad" as other sexual sins. Here's the finding: "Women, far more than men, are likely to act out their behaviors in real life, such as having multiple partners, casual sex, or affairs."[8] The Message version of Ecclesiastes 7:18 tells us that a man who fears God deals with all of reality. The reality is that porn is a deadly threat to intimacy, for both the man *and* the woman.

Bottom line? Porn doesn't love intimacy. It doesn't respect the sanctity of covenant sex. It wasn't created to bring two people closer together. It desecrates the sacredness of sex, and if you give it even a little of your self (body, mind, or spirit), it will fight until the death, with its "prize" being your soul, your relationship, your income . . . *you.*

I'm sure a lot of you are familiar with the story in Luke (11:17–26) that speaks of the corrupting spirit that was removed from someone and yet when it couldn't find anyone else to torment and possess, it went back to where it came from, bringing seven other spirits with it and leaving the person worse off than he was before. When it comes to pornography and the way it influences the lives of people, I think this story about sums it up. When you engage in porn of any kind—whether it's on DVD, on the internet, or even in books (and please believe, erotica fans, that I am getting to you before this chapter is out)—only heaven knows just how many foul spirits you are attaching to yourself.

Porn wasn't created to bring two people closer together.

The Effects

A couple of months ago, I was talking with a female married friend of mine about married sex and how it differs in so many ways from "single sex." Single sex can be so selfish: you have sex in your way on your terms. Single sex can be unrealistic: on so many levels the myth that ignorance (of your bad moods, bad habits, etc.) is bliss applies. And single sex is not ordained by God: "But fornication and all uncleanness or covetousness, let it not even be named among you, as is fitting for saints; neither filthiness, nor foolish talking, nor coarse jesting, which are not fitting, but rather giving of thanks" (Eph. 5:3–4 NKJV).

I remember chatting with a couple who at one time were in marital counseling but are now divorced. Like the wives who shared their testimonies in the previous chapter, they told me that when the Bible tells us you reap what you sow (Gal. 6:7–8), it means just that. When it comes to sexual sin, even if you have sex outside of marriage *and marry the person anyway*, there are still consequences to bear, some that can really throw you for a loop.

When I talked with a girlfriend about married sex after single sex, she agreed. One thing she and her husband enjoyed doing as singles was watching porn. When I asked her how it was affecting her married sex life now, I will never forget what she said: "Girl, sometimes it's like we have fifteen other people in bed with us due to all of the images we have seen."

First Corinthians 7:2 says, "Because sexual sin is a danger, *each man* should have his *own wife*, and *each woman* should have her *own husband*." God never wanted there to be physical *or* mental orgies in the marriage bed. When God said in Hebrews 13:4 that the marriage bed is undefiled, this means the marriage bed is pure. Porn may be a lot of things, but pure is not one of them!

Some of us have been taught—poorly, I might add—to fear the physical ramifications of premarital sex so much that we have forgotten that sex isn't just a physical act. Sure, porn won't get you pregnant. Porn won't even give you an STD (although I have another way of breaking down that acronym: Spiritually Transmitted Disease—and porn will give you a lethal case). But pornography can do just as much, if not more, damage. I liken it to a woman who is being emotionally abused versus a woman who is being physically abused. Sometimes, it's the scars you don't see that can affect you the most.

As for me and porn, my first introduction to it was with a guy I was sleeping with—well, having sex with because we hardly ever spent the night together—in college. One day, we decided to have sex at his friend's apartment and when I walked into the bedroom, there was a porn flick on the TV. Now in hindsight, I know that was a setup. He wanted me to see it. I also sense he probably wanted me to watch it to catch a few pointers because at the time, I wasn't as "skilled" as I think some of his other chicks were (he was a basketball player with a girlfriend and many other "friends").

For anyone who's never watched porn before (and if that is you, congratulations!), I'll give you a visual of a normal first reaction. My experience with porn was that initially it was a lot like looking at roadkill—and roadkill is disgusting. But it's also really shocking, in an oddly seductive kind of way. You just don't see stuff like that every day. When it came to porn, I had never seen two people having sex before, and so it felt like legal voyeurism. *Wow!* I thought. *I can sit and watch people have sex—all kinds of sex—and they don't mind.* This experience was the beginning of my off-and-on love/hate affair with porn for years to come.

I could watch people have sex and I did, and it appeared that the people on screen didn't mind (although we at XXXchurch have many testimonies of how many of these actors really felt after the cameras stop rolling). But here's the thing: I was never supposed to witness anyone having sex outside of the sex I will have with my future mate someday, and because I did, I have struggled in areas that I would have never predicted and God never intended. Watching other people having sex and reading about other people having sex have affected me sexually. There is an old proverb that states the eyes are the window to the soul. Don't take that as just a poetic line. When it comes to entertaining pornography, it's a warning.

Because I am a sexual being, moments come when I am tempted to have sex; sometimes due to temptation, other times I want it simply because my body says so (during ovulation is a really good example). Because I still see countless porn scenes in my head, on my "rough days" I'm tempted to look again. Come on, I write for a living and so I am on my PC every single day of my life. *Do you know how much free porn is on this thing?* Do you know how much I could watch without anyone knowing anything about it? And do you know how many times I have found myself asking these exact questions when my hormones are about to cuss me flat out?

So what keeps me from giving in? On some days it's nothing but the grace of God, a place I boldly go in time of need (Heb. 4:16). On others it's just being really real with myself about how much porn gives versus how much it takes.

Now I am about to get pretty graphic here, but you're a big girl, you can handle it. Besides, I already warned you that since the Enemy is so bold, it's time we get even bolder. One of my favorite Scriptures in the Bible is 1 Timothy 4:14–16. The Amplified

> *It's the scars you don't see that can affect you the most.*

Version tells us that when we share our testimony, tempered with our own personality, we save not only ourselves but also those who hear us. So let me share . . .

As often as I found porn to be erotically entertaining, one thing that helped me stop using it was how, more times than not, masturbating to pornography left me exhausted—literally. I mean worn out! I would watch a DVD for a couple of minutes, "handle myself," and then find myself falling to sleep . . . sometimes for a couple of hours on end. What made it worse was when I woke up, the first thing I wanted to do was watch more porn, masturbate again, and then that would cause me to go back to sleep again. It became a vicious cycle. Since then I have reached a conclusion with three main points.

Point #1: I don't have the time! According to a recent report on Census.gov, the average life expectancy for me, a black woman, is about seventy-seven years. When you take into account that six to eight hours of each day is spent sleeping and another eight to ten is spent working, I mean, do I really have time to lie around passed out from a two-minute round of porn? Isn't life too precious for that? I must admit that when I sit and just think about how much porn robbed me of time, that alone should be enough to keep me totally and forever free! But there were a few other things about it as well that brought me to a place of recovery.

Point #2: I don't have energy to waste! Over time, porn for me was becoming mentally exhausting as well. It's just really hard to get "enough." My first experience was watching a man and a woman. Soon I wanted to see two women and a man. Then it was two women. Then it was two men and a woman. Then it was orgies. When it comes to understanding the mentality of promiscuous men, porn helped me understand it better than I ever had before. I didn't have a stash of tapes I viewed over and over. Once I saw you a couple of times, I was ready to move on to someone else. That kind of brings me to point 3 about why I knew I needed to give it up.

Point #3: Porn has no redeeming value! Philippians 4:8 (NKJV) tells us: "Finally, brethren, whatever things are *true*, whatever things are *noble*, whatever things are *just*, whatever things are *pure*, whatever things are *lovely*, whatever things are of *good report*, if there is any *virtue* and if there is anything *praiseworthy*—meditate on these things." *Nothing about porn falls under these descriptives.*

But it goes deeper. I remember watching an HBO documentary on porn a couple of years ago. They interviewed some of the biggest "stars" in the industry. One very beautiful woman said, "Do you know how I have sex when I get home? On my back in the dark and I hope it's quick." Geez, and she was married! Another woman said, "It's a fantasy . . . scenes are chopped and edited. People don't see the real deal. You can't have sex on and on and on like you see on the screen."

True Reality

Remember how I mentioned the Scripture in Ecclesiastes that says a man who fears God deals with reality—all of it? Porn is so far from reality, it's ridiculous. It's designed to provide mental mirages. *Of course* the women are supposed to climax every time. *Of course* the guys are supposed to be ready. It's created to provide the illusion of people receiving lots of pleasure with little effort . . . or responsibility. But in my coming to terms with what it was doing to my body, mind, and soul, I had to accept two harsh realities—realities that outshone the fantasy that porn provides.

Violence against Women

First, how can I, as a woman, support the flesh-peddling of other women? Isn't that the ultimate example of not only hypocrisy but low self-worth? When Christ was on the earth, he said the second greatest commandment, after loving God with all of your mind, soul, and strength, is to love your neighbor as yourself (Luke 10:27). Women being used and abused for sex as I stand on the sidelines watching and cheering them on? That is sick. You know, I have friends who enjoy period films with gladiator scenes. Personally, I am not a big fan of violence and so I never understood how they could stomach all of the blood and gore that comes with that. But as I've been healing from porn and sexual misuse in general, I see that I was no better than they are or the people who, in Roman times, used to sit in the arenas and actually watch people be torn to shreds by other individuals and/or animals. A lot of us may not want to look at it from this perspective, but *porn is violent*. Violence can be defined as rough or injurious physical force, action, or treatment. It is an ultimate act of defilement and degradation against humanity, and when it comes to the focus of this particular book, against *women* in particular.

There's nothing gentle, loving, or caring about porn. People are in it to make money, and the Bible says that when it comes to the drive for being rich, money is a root of all sorts of evil (1 Tim. 6:10). Sexual immorality would definitely fall under that category. Therefore, how can I as a woman, first, and a follower of Christ, second (because the truth is that I am always a woman, but I don't always follow Christ's example), partake in something that encourages the rough and injurious treatment of other women?

I recall hearing a porn director say the only reason porn exists, in the high supply it does, is because of the demand for it. I have friends who love to complain about certain shows on television, but the thing is, they wouldn't know about them (to the degree they do) if they weren't watching them. Those shows wouldn't exist without viewer ratings. As the audience, we have a greater voice than we think.

There's nothing gentle, loving, or caring about porn.

So, one of the *first* reasons I gave up porn was because I couldn't continue to act as if the sexual abuse of women in that way was okay; I couldn't allow myself to use them to meet my sexual needs. To do so is cruel, vicious, mean, and violating, whether we ever meet face-to-face or not. In a sense I have been both the victim and the perpetrator of sexual abuse. If a woman, while having an orgasm, sat and watched a family member molest me, I would find that to be pure evil. For me to sit and watch a woman get pillaged by a man or some instrument is no different, no matter how much I may want to tell myself otherwise.

My Need to Be Detoxified

The second reason I gave up porn was that I had to get myself to a place where I detoxified the spirits of those porn people out of me. I will never forget a male friend of mine once telling me he had a dream that felt more like a nightmare. In his dream he was sitting in front of the television, masturbating to porn. When he ejaculated, the heads of his sperm had faces of the very women he was watching on the television screen. They had fangs and came right out and attacked his flesh and killed him. Unsettling, I know, but that's not too far from the truth of what porn actually does to the spirit of a person.

Just a couple of days before writing this chapter, I had a dream. I was riding in the car with a really popular rapper (who directed porn films for a season himself) and his friends. They told me I would have to help them rob some banks and convenience stores. When we got to a certain one, the rapper and I were outside standing watch while his friends went inside. Long story short, they were busted by the cops, but rather than the police arresting them and taking them in for questioning, they took the men's clothes off and raped them . . . right there in broad daylight. I was in shock. The rapper stood beside me with the sickest smirk on his face, like he enjoyed watching it. I woke up in the weirdest mood that lasted most of my day.

Thing is, I don't recall ever watching homosexual male pornography—ever. I have never been interested in it in the least. But porn takes us places we never wanted to go. Images are powerful, much more so than I think we give them credit or credence. We don't even realize the things that our subconscious holds on to. That's why we have to be so cautious of *everything* we take in. There were images in my head I didn't even know were there.

Second Corinthians 10:4–5 tells us: "We fight with weapons that are different from those the world uses. Our weapons have power from God that can destroy the Enemy's strong places. We destroy people's arguments and every proud thing that raises itself against the knowledge of God. *We capture every thought and make it give up and obey Christ.*" When I'm asked even now how I deal with all of the memories from my past sexual choices, I tell them it's a day-by-day, sometimes minute-by-minute, concerted effort. When a thought comes, I don't ignore it. I address it as something that is unhealthy for me and I replace it with something else. For instance, when I think about an old boyfriend, I will usually go and do something so opposite from the thought. Like laundry or something. No joke.

Erotica

Do you remember how one of the statistics stated that women tend to act on their sexual fantasies more than men? I had a lesbian experience in my teenage years (that I think was encouraged by seeds planted in my childhood), but for the most part my sexual experiences consisted of me and one man. *That's it.* However, I will tell you about a trap I found myself in, one that was very hard to escape. I started becoming desensitized to other kinds of sexual activity (three-ways and orgies, especially). I may not have done it myself, but I didn't mind watching it. Don't get too comfortable with this way of thinking. It's a setup.

While I'm here, let me address one of the more popular forms of pornography among women, one that many tend to justify as being okay: erotica. Thanks, Communitiesfor Decency.org, for providing me with some stats to support my case. According to the site:

> a comprehensive two-year study by Alexa Research, a leading web intelligence and traffic measurement service, has revealed . . . "sex" was the most popular term for which people searched. Of all the terms searched for online, 0.3289%—or roughly 1 of every 300 terms, were "sex." According to their online searching habits, people want "sex" more than they want "games," "music," "travel," "jokes," "cars," "jobs," "weather" and "health" combined. "Porn" (along with "porno" and "pornography") was the 4th most popular search term. "Nude" (and "nudes"), "xxx," "Playboy" and "erotic stories" (and "erotica") were also among the top 20.

Now, just so we're all clear, let me give the definition of *erotica*. It's basically any literature or art that's intended to arouse sexual desire. If you are a single woman, why would you want to be aroused in that way? So, my Zane fans, my Lora Leigh fans, my Trista Ann Michaels fans, my Violent Blue, Kimberly Zant, and Jackie Burton fans, you may have never watched a porn DVD in your life and you might be feeling pretty good about that, but reading graphic descriptions of sex is no better than watching people having sex. The Bible says that for every temptation, God provides a way of escape (1 Cor. 10:13). Please tell me how reading *Tempting the Beast* is helping you escape temptation.

Exactly.

When I was making my transition out of watching porn, I actually manipulated myself into believing that I could read erotic stories and "get away with it." But you know what? A lot of those stories had a deeper effect on me than some of the porn I've seen. Seemingly, the authors had to find a way to make reading about sex just as enticing as watching it. Because you don't have any images to go by when you are reading those stories, your mind can conjure up whatever kind of people you like, at any given time.

Proverbs 16:2 (NKJV) states, "All the ways of a man are pure in his own eyes, but the LORD weighs the spirits." Don't get caught up in the technicalities of your sins; watching but not doing, reading but not watching. At the end of the day, the same spirit, the spirit of Satan, is motivating it all.

The Enemy is very much like a drug dealer. Often a dealer will give you your first "hit" for free and then, once he gets you hooked, he starts to charge you. The "highs" of sexual immorality aren't much different. You watch one video . . . or two . . . or ten, and it seems like you are getting off scot-free. But there is a price to pay. Getting freed from porn is not easy. I know a woman who, for years, was so addicted to it that she started having her own teenage son go and pick up videos for her. It sounds disgusting, doesn't it? Yep, but to a certain extent I've been there. You get so caught up that you start telling yourself, *It's not as bad as actually* doing it. It is! I have images in my mind that I have to spend precious time casting down—images that never should have been there to begin with. I have seen body parts of both men and women that I never should have seen. I have seen acts that are totally degrading to the human body that I should have no earthly knowledge of. There are spirits that, to this day, try to haunt me (hence that dream) that never should have infiltrated my body, mind, and spirit to begin with.

Doing porn? Yep. That's bad. Watching porn? Reading erotica? In some ways that's worse because, again, people wouldn't be doing it (at least not to the degree they are) if we weren't demanding it. But the worst consequence of all? It's what Laci shared in her testimony: "It has definitely changed my relationship with God too. I feel more distant with Him and every time I want to talk to Him I feel guilty. Like I'm such a screw up and how could He still love me."

For the Enemy, when we get to this place, his mission is accomplished. God says in his Word that we are loved with an everlasting love (Jer. 31:3). This means that what he feels for us is boundless, ceaseless, constant—permanent. God loves us even while we're watching porn. God *is* love (1 John 4:8). Love is simply who he is.

But the Enemy is fully aware of how feeling separated from that love can affect our thoughts, our emotions, and eventually our actions. Sin is meant to separate us. And when we go back to the purpose of sex, to bring about marital oneness and unity, porn would be one of the ultimate tricks and deterrents of that purpose, wouldn't it?

What to Do?

You're tempted.

You watch two (or more) other people having sex for money.

You have sex with yourself while watching it.

You feel guilty for watching the sex and masturbating.

You do the cycle all over again.

Where is the love in that? Where is God's purpose for sex in that? *Where is the good in that?*

My Vagina's Monologue

- - - - - - - - - - -

No doubt the title of the following poem caught your atten-
tion. It was written by a friend of mine who is a virgin but who
sometimes struggles with remaining that way. I find it to be a
poignant yet comedic look at what goes on when the mind
battles it out: to wait or not to wait.

I've been down here in seclusion for so long,
I wonder if I can bounce back
My owner has been tripping lately and won't cut me no
    slack
She got her head caught up in that Book she deems to
    be a major deal,
I just want a head caught up on my hook,
Pardon me for a second, do you mind if I keep it real?
I'm feigning for some attention, I need a connection
I need some interaction, I ain't afraid of protection
But she keeps imposing these random injections
Whenever I get the body to say okay, her mouth reneges
    and says no
It's thoroughly pissing me off and in a minute I'm about
    to blow
She so up and down, she got me going through the
    changes
Every time I set something up,
she reads something then comes back and rearranges
Who does she think she is, does she know who I am?
I am what make her who is she is
and here she is disregarding me like spam

I feel like there's no respect and she never hears me out
Whenever I try to speak she shushes me at the mouth
Me and the rest of the body are thinking about going on
strike
Cuz we'd be messed up if she think
this is how we're going to live out the rest of our life
I overheard her telling somebody the other day,
that she no longer thinks she's ready for marriage
I almost had a conniption right then and there,
And was tempted to close down shop
to spare any future embarrassment
Out of all the vaginas out there, I'm the only one not
being used
I'm filing a complaint to the vagina authorities
because this has got to be vagina abuse
She taking this virtuous thing a little too far
And her purity aspect is set way above any bar
All I wanna do is get what's rightfully mine
But she keep replying "in due time"
Time is due now, matter of fact, time is past due
Who ever "in due time" is, I can't wait to get my hands on
you
And if she read another piece of literature,
ask for more strength from her Savior,
thumb through another page of that Book,
or continually change her behavior
I'll just go silent
She won't hear a peep out of me
I'll just sit back and see what "waiting" allots me to see
Whatever it is, it better be right
It better be the best that she's never had or we gonna
fight
Because I personally think this waiting thing ain't polite
But since this is what she wants to do,
I'll just sit tight

©Kenitra "Neechiwoo" Woods, 2009

Overexposure

Media and Sexuality

It is not fancy hair, gold jewelry, or fine clothes that should make you beautiful. No, your beauty should come from within you—the beauty of a gentle and quiet spirit that will never be destroyed and is very precious to God.

1 Peter 3:3–4

In the media, accomplishing beauty can simply mean a mere wave of an airbrush correcting what is flawed; but in the real world, innermost beauty is perfectly flawless.

Vanese Henley, author

The day before I sat down to pen this chapter, a girlfriend of mine and I were talking about this billboard for a certain alcoholic beverage that we both find to be cool. Now that's an entirely different book: discussing what I think about drinking things that do not come in Tropicana cartons or

Sonic Styrofoam cups—although I will say that contrary to a lot of sermons that I've heard, the Bible doesn't speak against *consuming* alcohol so much as *being consumed by* it (see Prov. 20:1; 31:6; Eccles. 9:7; 10:19). Yet and still, because I have heard more war stories than love stories about the effects of alcohol, I will refrain from giving this certain brand a straight-out plug. I will, however, tell you what the billboard says, although it's somewhat paraphrased because I haven't seen it in about six weeks or so: "Sex sells. But we don't need sex to sell this."

Oh, if I could get that quote printed on shirts and put them on the back of every woman in America, I would—and someday, I might just try! Yes, it may be a current fact that sex sells, but it shouldn't, and it's time that we stop accepting that it does. It's time that we put sex back where it belongs—not with a price tag but in the hands of those who "rock gold" (or silver) bands on the third finger of their left hand.

In my day, if people wanted porn, they would have to go to the other side of town.

Not too long ago I was engaged in another conversation, this time with my mother, about what it must be like to raise children in the current state of this society. She said, "The Bible says there is nothing new under the sun [Eccles. 1:9], but in my day, even when *you* were little, if people wanted porn, they would have to go to the other side of town, be a certain age, and pay for it in a store. Now children can download it on the internet, see sex scenes on regular sitcoms, and look at nearly naked women on billboards. I don't know what I would do if I had to raise you in all of that and still have to tell you not to think about sex."

As a teen mom mentor, I'm here to tell you it's no easy task. No easy task at all. *Inundated* is putting it mildly when it comes to all that young people have to deal with on a daily basis, especially when it comes to the influence of pop culture, namely, music. Now, as a woman who *loves* music *and* the culture of hip-hop (which often gets a bad rap), let me just say that rap music is not the cause of all that's evil in music or pop culture. Whether it's the lyrics or the videos you catch on MTV or BET (when they actually show videos!), no matter what the genre, sexuality seems to be compromised.

The Bible says that death and life are in the power of the tongue (Prov. 18:21) and love of money is a root of all sorts of evil (1 Tim. 6:10). Just because we may choose to ignore God's instructions (and warnings) doesn't make them any less real or applicable. The Word of God also says that we all will reap what we have sown and that when we sow to the flesh, we will reap corruption (Gal. 6:7–8). I wanted to quote some lyrics of popular songs on the Billboard 100—songs that are in regular radio rotation—but my publisher said they were too graphic to print, so I will just leave it at this: crass lyrics about women's body parts, the intimacy that takes place between a man and a woman, or pursuing a woman in a way that sounds more like a rapist than a gentleman— none of these are edifying to women, the very people God put on this earth to be blessings and helpers to men and to add favor to their lives (see Prov. 18:22).

Overused

Aside from writing books, touring with XXXchurch, and mentoring pregnant teens, I also do some freelance journalism writing, which means I get exposed to a lot of information. Not very long ago a certain female R&B singer, whom I find to be pretty close to physically stunning, had some naked pictures "leaked" onto the internet. I put "leaked" in quotes because she took some of the shots of herself with her cell phone, and so I'm not clear about who really posted them for the world to see. Either way, it was very sad to witness such a thing. As beautiful as her body seemed, when I looked at the shots of her, I literally wept for her inside. With all of the fame, all of the endorsement deals, all the compliments and accolades that she receives for her outer beauty, it would appear that in Hollywood she has not learned one very important thing: she doesn't have to show her body for her self-worth to be revealed.

Not surprisingly, the existence of the photos stayed in the news for only a couple of days, because the truth is that most of us have gotten so used to nudity that it doesn't faze us. Today I sat and thought about how many body parts of women I had seen since this morning, whether it was in a magazine, on television, or online, and after around noon, I lost count. If it's not the cleavage, it's the stomach. If it's not the stomach, it's legs. Why would our young women want to cover up when all the celebrities whom they look up to are doing just the opposite?

Sadly, it doesn't stop at the outfits, or lack thereof. A couple of months ago I checked out a riveting documentary, *America, the Beautiful* by filmmaker Darryl Roberts. It's so full of information, I really encourage you to Google the flick and check it out for yourself. My point in bringing it up is that we have gotten to a place where showing what *we've got* isn't enough. Now many women are at a point where they want to create in themselves what someone else has and then flaunt that. The documentary featured a segment in which women are changing the way their labia look. They may see a woman in porn, for example, and decide, *I want mine to look like that.* Am I serious?! Very.

Recently I read an article in *Essence* magazine that echoed this trend. The article was entitled "The Body Shop" and the subtitle asked, "How far would you go to get a man—or please the one you have?"[1] It went on to share how women are trying pole dancing, paying for sex lessons (huh?), and undergoing black-market surgical enhancements all in the pursuit of sexual perfection. One stat revealed that almost 10,000 buttock enhancements were performed in 2007, and one woman shared that her boyfriend suggested she study some porno films so she could learn some skills to better please him.

Now, that really disgusted me, but just to make sure that my current lifestyle (abstinence) wasn't making me prudish or hypersensitive, I did a quiet run-through of the covers of the women's magazines that were out the same month of that *Essence* issue. *Cosmo*'s cover story was "What He Thinks of Your Orgasm Noises." The magazine *W* focused on the subject "Hot Love" with actress Ginnifer Goodwin in, I think, umm, some underwear. *Glamour* featured "New Sex Secrets Guys Keep," and I won't even get into what the men's magazines had to share.

Geez. Talk about overexposed! And we wonder why we have sexual image issues. Just to make sure it wasn't an off week (yeah, right), I reviewed some stats on sexuality and the media as well. It wasn't an off week, unfortunately. Although these stats reflect how television is affecting the sexuality of teenagers, I think it's worth mentioning because personally, I'm not really sure when you are ever "grown enough" to be promiscuous or to have sex outside of God's will.

Anyway, according to ParentsTV.org, RAND, a nonprofit analysis group, conducted a study that was published in the September 2004 issue of *Pediatrics*, which stated,

A study of 1792 adolescents ages 12–17 showed that watching sex on TV influences teens to have sex. *Youths who watched more sexual content were more likely to initiate intercourse and progress to more advanced noncoital sexual activities in the year following the beginning of the study.* Youths in the 90th percentile of TV sex viewing had a predicted probability of intercourse initiation that was approximately double that of youths in the 10th percentile. *Basically, kids with higher exposure to sex on TV were almost twice as likely than kids with lower exposure to initiate sexual intercourse* [emphasis added].

No wonder!

According to SexInfoOnline, about 66 percent of prime-time shows contain some sexual content; the Kaiser Family Foundation has reported that 80 percent of the content presented on soap operas is sexual in nature. Greenberg and Woods reported an average of 6.6 sex acts in each soap opera hour, and the bulk of the sexual action and language occurs between unmarried characters. One study found that unmarried heterosexual characters engage in sexual intercourse *four to eight times more than* married characters.[2] Oh, we've come a long way from when America was shocked by the premier of *The Brady Bunch*, a married couple with six children, who actually opted to share a bed rather than sleep separately in two twin-sized beds.

Now it makes sense why God instructed us to think on what's noble, just, pure, and lovely, doesn't it (Phil. 4:8)? The Bible says that the devil is the prince of the air (Eph. 2:2) and the father of lies (John 8:44). If we're not careful, we can begin to take in so much of this stuff that we start thinking this is the way life is meant for us to live. Just because it is popular doesn't mean it's a part of God's original design for our quality of life. And when it comes to sexuality, Hebrews 13:4 clearly states that it is only the marriage bed that is pure; fornication and adultery are not. It also makes clear why we must keep God and his Word in the forefront of our minds on a daily basis (Matt. 6:11). If we don't and continue to let these kinds of songs, articles, and images overtake our mind, body, and spirit, we will begin to forget God's purpose for our body and our self.

We Are What We Think

This is not my PSA (public service announcement) to watch TBN marathons for the rest of your life or throw out all of your secular CDs (c'mon now). I am saying that what you may consider to be "harmless entertainment" may be what's seducing your spirit, ultimately doing your self-image harm. Proverbs 23:7 (NKJV) clearly tells us that as a man thinks in his heart, so is he. What is in your "heart space"? *The Young and the Restless* or the story of Ruth? *Cosmo*'s advice on how to please your man or Song of Solomon, which embraces and celebrates sex between two loving covenant partners? When you think about sex and sexuality, are you tempted to compete and compare with what some random, strange, self-titled "sexpert" tells you to do? Or do you ponder the kind of love we all deserve—the kind of love that God says his daughters should wait for?

A couple of years ago I interviewed a "sex expert" for an article on sexual fulfillment. I loved his approach to the issue: "Young men learn about sex from porn and young women learn from women's magazines. You put those two people in the dark and all you get is one big mess." For the most part, he's so right.

God knows me and my future mate better than any sex therapist.

Frankly I never really understood why we would trust the "insight" of some magazine written by someone who doesn't know us personally and is paid to produce that kind of copy. The Bible says that if I acknowledge God in all of my ways, he will direct my path (Prov. 3:5–6). God knows me and my future mate better than any sex therapist. I think I'll save my five dollars and wait on God to give me the inside scoop that I need. Which is kind of the whole point of this chapter.

Earlier this year, I started two blogs for singles who desire to be married someday. One is called, "So, How Did YOU Know?" and the other is entitled, "Before You Jump the Broom" (you can check them both out at blogspot: http://missnosipho.gather.com/). Anyway, the first one currently contains posts from more than seventy people speaking on how they knew their spouse was the one for them; what they love about their covenant partner's mind, body, and spirit; and advice for singles as it relates to the lessons they learned within their own marriage. I will never forget what a man by the name of Melvin said when I asked him what he loved most about his wife's body: "I love that when God created her, he had me in mind."

Sadly, you probably won't find that kind of statement in any magazine in your favorite drugstore, but that's just what God wants all of his daughters to hear—from their husband. When I was having sex, because I was living my life according to the wisdom of the world, I let myself fall victim to a lot of what people claimed was sexy, desirable, and physically beneficial to men. Once I came out of that filth, I began to understand what God meant when he said that before the womb, I was called and chosen (Jer. 1:5) and what he does lasts forever and nothing can be added to or taken from it (Eccles. 3:14).

Before the womb, he called me to be someone special for someone special, and once I am united with that person, it will be so in the will of God, I won't need a breast job, sex lessons, *Cosmo* tips, or soap opera insights to please him. I will be his God-ordained helper. With the help of God, that will be more than enough. Ladies, we have to get to a place where we purge ourselves of the lies we have been told. John 8:44 describes the Enemy as the father of lies. Anything that causes you to devalue who you are, anything that encourages you to question your worth as an individual, is a lie.

More Than Enough

So what should we be focusing on? The lead Scripture for this chapter is a good start.

The week I penned this was the week that a magazine I freelance for published my article "The Mouths of Men," in which I interviewed two of my male friends. They shared what attracts them to a woman and what will hold their attention beyond that initial attraction. Both of them said that they found someone who is ladylike to be really captivating.

That makes sense. They're made in the image of God, and God's Word tells us it's not what we put on that makes us beautiful; it's the quiet and gentle spirit, which will never be destroyed, that's truly precious to God (1 Peter 3:3–4). I don't know about you, but I want to be married one time and one time only, forever. Hearing about what a godly man finds to be "marriage material" is definitely getting me closer to my mark.

Personally I find beauty to be a gift just like writing, singing, or preaching. Halle Berry? Yeah, she's beautiful. Salma Hayek? Yep, she's beautiful too. Jennifer Lopez, Jessica Alba, Jessica Biel, Scarlett Johansson, Kim Kardashian, Jill Scott, Naomi Campbell, Megan Fox? Beautiful, beautiful, beautiful, and yet they've all had issues with men (who hasn't?). When it comes to beautiful women, it's actually one of my male friends (shout-out to AG) who says it best: "The finest woman in the world right now is probably getting on some man's last nerve!"

> *It's not what we put on that makes us beautiful; it's the quiet and gentle spirit that's truly precious to God.*

Don't let the media hype, hype you. I remember doing an article on "counterfeits" and looking up synonyms for the word on www.dictionary.com. You will never guess what I found. *Hollywood!* In a sense, that's what 1 Corinthians 1:20–21 says: "Where is the wise person? Where is the educated person? Where is the skilled talker of this world? God has made the wisdom of the world foolish. In the wisdom of God the world did not know God through its own wisdom. *So God chose to use the message that sounds foolish to save those who believe.*"

To be the kind of woman who is more focused on developing her character than removing her cellulite. To be the kind of woman who loves with her heart more than she wants to be loved for her looks. To be the kind of woman who wants her husband to receive, in every sense, what he is deserving of (which includes seeing her breasts, her upper thighs, her buttocks, and so on)—that is a woman worthy to be praised.

These days I don't have to look like I belong on the cover of a magazine. As long as my future husband's eyes gleam when he sees me, that's all the spotlight I need!

When Sex Is Your Drug

- - - - - - - - - - -

"I've been walking with the Lord since last July. I've known about Him all my life, but chose to follow my own path for 12 years. During that time, I started reading erotica, which eventually turned into viewing porn. There came a point when the words no longer 'satisfied' me. Eventually that escalated to 'regular' porn no longer being enough and the level of depravity I required sickens me to think about now. It does not consume my thoughts, or affect any other part of my life, when I'm out and socializing. However, when I get home, and I'm alone, the temptation to view porn is there. I'm active in my church, do volunteer work with domestic abuse victims, and work in health care. No one looking at me would ever know I have this struggle, and I really don't want them to know.

"Before I got baptized last year, I had been involved in a few relationships with men, all of them sexual, and quite frankly I miss sex! I sometimes wish I had a drinking or a drug problem. It would be so much easier for me to cry out to the Lord and ask that He take away my desire for alcohol or drugs. However, I don't want to ask Him to take away my desire for companionship and sex. It's not an unnatural thing. It's not a desire I want removed. I know that it may never be in God's plan for me to marry, but I'm seriously struggling with that. I often think that if I wasn't trying to live a godly life, I would be 'dating' someone now and would have an outlet for my sexual desire. So my question is, as a single person, how do I get to the point where I put Him first? How do I get to where I no longer turn to porn or erotica to bring me a tangible release, when prayer doesn't work? Right now I'm stuck in a cycle of praying for strength, masturbating, feeling guilt/disgust, and then praying for forgiveness. I would love some insight on how other singles deal with this. I've been reading a few posts and answers on this site, but can't seem to find an answer to how to deal with simply missing sex. Specific Scripture would be very helpful."

Anonymous, an XXXchurch.com blog reader

- - - - - - - - - -

Confusion

The Misuse of Sex

You were bought at a price; do not become slaves of men.

1 Corinthians 7:23 NKJV

Abuse [is] like laudanum: you have to double the dose as the sensibilities decline.

Harriet Beecher Stowe, author

About three years before I penned *Inside of Me*, God gave me a term to describe the kind of lifestyle I was engaging in when it came to my sexuality. It's "sexual misuse." My original definition was "sex outside of God's intention." However, I remember doing an interview on a local television show and the host said, "So, when you separate the difference between sexual *abuse* and sexual *misuse*, would it be that one is what's done *to* you while the other is what you do *to yourself*?" *Ding, ding, ding.* That is perfect.

- -

This chapter is going to address *sexual misuse* in a way that *Inside of Me* couldn't, because, to be honest, I was still caught up in it at the time. Up until 2007, the longest I had been abstinent since becoming sexually active in 1993 was ten months. All that Word . . . all that wisdom . . . and I still couldn't get the sex monkey off my back. *What was that about?*

Well, the thing is, when it comes to obeying God, we have to do it 100 percent. You can be living 99.9 percent truth, and that fraction of a lie can destroy your life. The lie that tripped me up more than anything was my cyclic state of self-manipulation and rationalization, the crazed voice inside me that said, "Well, since we all make mistakes, tripping over my discernment and into a man's arms and ultimately his sheets, every once in a while, isn't all that bad." Especially if I loved him . . . especially if he was my boyfriend. Whatever. The devil is a liar.

I recall not too long ago hearing a sermon in which the pastor said that even partial or incomplete obedience is total disobedience, and he's right. When it came to my getting freed from my sexual misuse cycle, every few years or so, when I would find myself with another broken heart or unplanned pregnancy, the Holy Spirit would gently lead me to the following Scripture:

> He also spoke this parable: "A certain man had a fig tree planted in his vineyard, and he came seeking fruit on it and found none. Then he said to the keeper of his vineyard, 'Look, for three years I have come seeking fruit on this fig tree and find none. Cut it down; why does it use up the ground?' But he answered and said to him, '*Sir, let it alone this year also, until I dig around it and fertilize it. And if it bears fruit, well. But if not, after that you can cut it down.*'"
>
> Luke 13:6–9 NKJV

I knew what God wanted of me: one year. I needed to be abstinent for one solid year. Like Esther, who spent a year getting ready for her king (Esther 2:12–13), for me to reach my destiny, I needed to purge fornication from my system for twelve solid months.

There have been and I pray will continue to be times in my life when I know (that I know that I know) that God spoke something specifically to me. Undoubtedly, through those verses of Scripture in Luke, this was one of those times. Matthew 12:33 tells us that a tree is known by its fruit, right? Well, as much as I wanted to deny it, when it came to character development, I've always known full well that one of the fruit of the Spirit is self-control (Gal. 5:22–23). What I also knew is that it was a fruit I didn't really want to partake of; I didn't *want* to control myself, especially in the realm of sexuality. Again, God knew it, I knew it, and Satan knew it, and let me tell you something: when it comes to knowing something that's best for you and ignoring it, especially when it's a revelation from God, that's a surefire way to keep you from truly fulfilling your purpose and receiving access to all of the good plans that God has for your life (Jer. 29:11). God withholds *no good thing* from those *who walk uprightly* (Ps. 84:11). And now, more than ever, I'm sure that's why the Enemy wants to keep us single gals on our backs!

Sex outside of God's plan doesn't give us anything; it takes.

Sex outside of God's plan doesn't *give* us anything; it takes. The initial title of *Inside of Me* was *Queens Can't Balance Crowns on Their Backs* because the truth is, if you're a single woman of royalty (1 Peter 2:9), no matter how hard you may try, when it comes to "balancing" sexual immorality with virtue, it just doesn't work. If you're even half as biblically conscious as God has created you to be, you will fall on your face, in repentance to the Lord, for doing what was blatantly against his will, *every single time*. A lukewarm lifestyle, even and especially when it comes to sexual sin, does not please God (see Rev. 3:16). It never has and it never will.

Godly Purpose

So what do I believe is a part of my destiny . . . the godly good plans . . . *my purpose?* Okay, I don't want to seem like one of those psycho self-prophesiers who really end up being prophe-*liars*, but I do believe that someday God will bless me with the ordained-by-him roles of being a wife and mother. I once read that R&B singer Jill Scott was quoted as saying, "To be the queen of a household is a powerful thing," and I would totally agree. But to be *that kind of queen*, God must prepare us. Personally, when it comes to getting to my "Proverbs 31 Promised Land," I often tell the story of sitting at the wedding of someone significantly younger than me—with a full-fledged attitude. "God, she's a kid! Why is *she* getting married before *I* am?"

God is about keeping his Word, and he is very clear about the consequences that come with our unhealthy choices. James 1:14–16 states: "But people are tempted when their own evil desire leads them away and traps them. This desire leads to sin, and then the sin grows and brings death. My dear brothers and sisters, do not be fooled about this."

Death. It manifests in many forms. Obviously, my sexual sin didn't result in the loss of my life (praise God), but it did cause the loss of four of my children, the brokenness of my spirit, the damage to my self-esteem, and an extreme case of "blurriness" when it came to seeing and receiving the vision that God has for me. Just like when the Woman ate of the fruit and lived to tell about it, *while still suffering for her sins*, any time we operate outside of God's love—the very thing that holds his plans for us—there is a kind of death that comes on us because, apart from the Lord, *we can do nothing* (John 15:5). This includes remaining spiritually healthy while doing things that are physically not.

You can't do something with your body without it affecting your mind. You can't think something with your mind that does not also affect your spirit. Anytime you have sex, *everything about you is affected*, changed . . . and from a spiritual place, if it's outside of covenant, to a certain extent, everything about you gets damaged. That's why I find the term "safe sex" to be a joke. The only "safe sex" is in marriage (because abstinence isn't "safe sex," it's just obedience).

Actually, even when I was having sex, I believed this to be true, but I came across an article that really brought it home for me. Not too long ago, *Essence* magazine ran a story about a man who had herpes but still continued to have unprotected sex while not telling his partners for fear of rejection. I'm sure the natural (worldly) resolution to the problem would be to always make sure that a man puts on a condom, right? But you see that's just it: why do people use condoms? To protect themselves, right? Now, I am not speaking to married people who may be using it as a form of birth control. But when you are single, the moment you think you are ready to have sex with someone and you decide to use a condom, there should be something that goes off in your head that says, *If I need to protect myself from you physically—whether it be from pregnancy or an STD—then I need to protect myself holistically and not have sex with you* at all! Talk about condoms. Until someone can come up with a fail-safe *heart condom* (and they won't!), sex outside of marriage should always, without a doubt, forever and always, be totally out of the question!

The only "safe sex" is in marriage.

Whether we choose to acknowledge it or not, whether we have seen immediate ramifications of it or not, sin is detrimental to our health and, if we partake of it long enough, one way or another, *it will kill us*. It's just that simple. I believe God was telling me at my friend's wedding that in my choosing not to wait for his best, I was delaying the time in receiving it, because every man whom I compromised myself with ended up leaving me wounded, which in turn took more time for me to heal. It's hard, and in many ways not even fair, to unite a healthy, living spirit to a broken, dead one; to put a spiritually whole person with someone who is choosing to remain sexually compromised.

Not too long ago I was writing an article that called for me to look up the definition of the word *death*. Do you know that it is described (among other things) as "insensitive"? *Dead* and *insensitive* are stepbrothers. Wow. Now, think about that and look again at the James 1:14–16 passage, only with the "Shellie-remix-translation" this time: "But *single women* are tempted when their own *lust* leads them away and traps them. This *want* leads to *separation from God's love and protection*, and then the *separation* grows and brings *insensitivity*. My dear brothers and sisters, do not be fooled about this."

Sin causes death. Sin makes people insensitive. And what happens when a person becomes insensitive? Over time, it takes more and more to make them feel, right? When it comes to being "sexually insensitive," check out a Scripture that is sure to blow your mind:

> This I say, therefore, and testify in the Lord, that you should no longer walk as the rest of the Gentiles walk, in the futility of their mind, having their understanding darkened, being alienated from the life of God, because of the ignorance that is in them, because of the blindness of their heart; *who, being past feeling, have given themselves over to lewdness, to work all uncleanness with greediness.*
>
> Ephesians 4:17–19 NKJV

Spiritual Desensitization

Some of us go to church every week. We know what the Word of God says about sexual immorality. We have been damaged by sex outside of God's will—and we know it—more times than we care to count. And still, we continue to have sex outside of covenant. Could hell be an ultimate consequence of sexual sin? According to the Bible, that would be a definite yes (Jude 7). However, let me provide you with another perspective of hell—right here on earth.

A man by the name of Tryon Edwards was once quoted as saying, "Hell is truth seen too late." Some of us know what it's like to have the spiritual aftertaste of hellfire and brimstone being shoved down our throats every Sabbath or Sunday, but let me show you hell with a twist. The Bible says that when we know the truth, we are made free (John 8:32), right? The Bible also says that confession brings about healing (James 5:16), right? If you want to avoid the hell that sexual sin brings, you have to know the truth, be open to living it, and be honest with yourself about it. *The truth* is that some of us have been sexually misusing ourselves for so long we have become *insensitive* to what it is doing to our mind, soul, and spirit and how it is affecting the lives of others, because, indeed, we are called to love our neighbors as ourselves!

Now chances are this is not totally our fault. As a matter of fact, rarely is this ever the case. As for me, sexual abuse lay the groundwork for my sexual misuse. The wounds of a family member taking advantage of me, and then not letting those wounds heal properly, definitely caused me to lose some "heart feeling" in the places where a woman should be the most responsive. But when I make the time to think about all that happened to me since the age of fifteen, I have to take some real responsibility and ownership for my actions. Sexual abuse may have been *a part* of my sexuality foundation, but through my own choices in my adult years (I started having sex a couple of months before my nineteenth birthday), I definitely "built the building." It wasn't until I completed a year of abstinence (currently going into year three) that I was able to see what I was building for what it really was: a really sick habit that was slowly but surely ruining my life.

For those of you having a hard time even wanting to give up fornication, doing it, setting it out, sleeping around, making love—or whatever else you are calling your sexual situation—let me pause right here for a moment. I know what it's like to hear sermons or read books by Christians who try to encourage abstinence while claiming either, 1) that they have remained sexually pure, or 2) if they did have sex, they didn't like it. *I'm not that gal.* I love sex. I enjoy sex. I miss sex dearly. That's not the point or issue here. The point is that I should have never found myself in a place where I can say that I love it, enjoy it, miss it. As I am going through my abstinence journey, if there is one consequence I never saw coming, it was the torment of starting and stopping something that God never intended to have end once it was introduced into my life.

Through Paul, God instructed married people not to withhold sex from one another (1 Cor. 7:5). That leads me to believe that God knew sex was a habit that would, and should, be very hard to break. Learning how to be abstinent in my mid-30s, no doubt, was never a part of God's perfect will for my life, and when I speak on sexual misuse, I often share that as being one of the hardest pills to swallow. A part of the "torture" that comes with having sex outside of marriage is stopping something that God wanted to be continuous in my life—once I started having it with my husband. Girl, I tell you, while I can give you a billion reasons going without until marriage is best (and I will try to share a few in an upcoming chapter), I can also tell you that giving up this particular habit can be one of the roughest things you will ever do. I understand substance abuse recovery, as best as I can, on an entirely different level now.

As a matter of fact, I have some family members who are recovering substance abusers. They have good days and they have bad days and sometimes the effort to resist their drug of choice is a moment-by-moment thing. Let me tell you something: it wasn't until I really decided to go without sex for more than ten months that I could not only sympathize but *empathize* with what they are going through. Some days I am on my face in tears trying to go without, answering an email from my favorite past "hit" (I'm just being real), or avoiding "eating ice cream," which is what an email buddy of mine calls masturbation. Some days, seemingly out of nowhere, I have the extreme urge to check out a porn clip or two (I still remember the names of some sites from back in the day) or to flirt more than I should with a cute guy who comes on to me. Oh, to get away from the highs that once consumed me.

My father is a recovering substance abuser, and although his lifestyle irks me to no end at times, I see there is a lesson in all of the information God has allowed me to discover by observ-

God instructed married people not to withhold sex from one another.

ing him. I see what my dad goes through and it's a reminder to me on a consistent basis that alcohol and drugs are not something that I want to get into, no matter how intriguing they may be at times. Reality is: it hurts my father; he struggles.

If you happen to be a virgin reading this, let me be a spiritual sister and counselor for you, a living example of why sex outside of marriage does not need to be your "drug of choice," either. That's not to say that you do not struggle in your own way, but this side of sex contains the consequences of not being covered. What you are currently experiencing is a natural desire, as a sexual being, for sex. That's *very different* from detoxing from the abuse of it. Please don't test it out to see if I'm wrong. Trust me, I'm not.

Spiritual Incest

When I had finally gotten to a place where I really wanted to take the abstinence thing seriously, I asked God how he sees sexual misuse, why he finds it so deplorable. I heard God saying back to me, "Well Shellie, to be honest with you, I don't want you to sleep with your brother. I want you to sleep with your husband. In this life, you are to see people as your brothers and sisters in Christ. The only thing that changes that in my eyes is marriage."

Wow. Okay. No wonder the Message version of 1 Corinthians 6:16 tells us: "Sex is as much spiritual mystery as physical fact." Marriage changes the entire dynamic between two people. Leviticus 18 breaks it down—and quite thoroughly, I might add—telling who are not supposed to have sexual relations with one another. Verse 6 pretty much covers it: "You must never have sexual relations with your close relatives. I am the LORD." I know this applies to relationships in the natural, but there are all kinds of Scriptures that describe men and women as brothers and sisters in the spiritual as well (1 Cor. 7:15; James 2:15, for example). So, basically, since it's only within the sanctity of marriage that the Bible acknowledges two people as being one, and since it's that transition (and that transition alone) that makes two individuals husband and wife (Matt. 19:5–6), I get where God is coming from. If you are having sex without being one, without being husband and wife, then in the spirit realm, you are still brother and sister—you are close family relatives, and (dum, de, dum, dum), you are committing *spiritual incest*.

Ewwwwh, right? Sorry. But with this perspective thrown into the mix, it is clear why sex outside of marriage is so despicable to God. I don't know about you, but when I first read the story of Lot's daughters plotting to get pregnant by their father (Gen. 19:30–38), I wanted to hurl, both naturally and spiritually. However, when I look at what I've done with the past fourteen sex partners I've had, while plotting to get pregnant was never in the plans, what I did wasn't much better. I considered myself to be a part of God's family and most of the men I've been with considered themselves to be the same (I won't even get into the risks I subjected myself to by sleeping with men who didn't . . . whole nother book!). So that means we are brothers and sisters in Christ. I sleep with him, outside of marriage, when he is my brother—spiritual incest, indeed.

I don't really know how to make it any plainer. Fornication is not some "little sin" we commit. Fornication is the opposite of what God intended for sex to be. It's illegal activity. It's against his will, way, and purpose for our lives, and when we do it, it's a form of self-abuse—it's sexual misuse. I'm sure some of you are wondering how I stopped, especially with it being such a lifelong struggle of mine. We'll get to that in chapter 9. In the meantime, as you move into the next chapter, I ask you to enter into it with a repentant heart. You are no longer ignorant about the magnitude of what you are doing, and God is going to hold you accountable for it.

After leaving my last sex partner, I remember hearing God say, "You know what your problem is? You believe in my love but you don't believe in my wrath. *They are both very real.*" Then he led me to the following Scripture:

> Do not worship idols, as some of them did. Just as it is written in the Scriptures: "They sat down to eat and drink, and then they got up and sinned sexually." We must not take part in sexual sins, as some of them did. *In one day twenty-three thousand of them died because of their sins.* We must not test Christ as some of them did; they were killed by snakes. Do not complain as some of them did; they were killed by the angel that destroys.
>
> 1 Corinthians 10:7–10

God is a man of his word and his Word. Please, if you are caught up in the cycle of sexual misuse, take this as a mental caution light and *stop!* Trying to speed ahead could cause trouble on levels you never anticipated.

God knows it. Satan knows it.

That should be heads-up enough.

A Letter
to My Former Self

- - - - - - - - - -

Baby Girl,

I know you're nervous.

The man you've loved since ever knowing what love was, you will be seeing in just a couple of days—and at a *wedding*, on *his birthday*, no less.

Oh, how life is full of so many ironies and surprises. Back when you were nineteen and giddy (or was it delusional?), you and "he" used to tease his cousin about how selfish he was, how immature he was, how "so-not-husband-potential" he was. And now, fourteen years later, in a race to the altar, he has beat you both to the winning line, marrying a woman who is tall in stature (literally) and character.

But that's not what tops the list of ironies or surprises when it comes to this situation. What you really didn't expect was that you two would be attending these nuptials apart. Sure, "he" will be at the altar, but as a groomsman and not the groom. Yes, you will be walking down the aisle, but not in white—lavender—and not as the bride but a guest.

To add insult to injury, after not speaking for over ten years, two years ago, he reached out to apologize for writing a nightmare ending to your storybook romance. Oh, and Baby Girl, what did you do? Instead of closing the chapter of this passionately tumultuous novella, novel, book series, you pulled out another page of your heart and started dreaming, wishing, and hoping again. A two-hour luncheon turned into a twenty-four-month reunion tour of "The Way We Were." What was supposed to be an "I'm sorry" translated into "I still love you and I always will."

– – – – – – – – – –

Baby Girl, until you heard it again, you didn't even realize it was something you had so deeply longed for since the last time you heard his voice. Like a woman in search of the right shoe, you tried on the words of others, but nothing else quite fit. You always seemed to grow a deafened ear to what usually followed those sentiments: "I can't be what you want, need, or deserve. This won't work."

I know you're disappointed. Baby Girl, I hate to say it, but I'm a little disappointed *in you*. Not because you took a chance on love—that's what living life is all about—but because you were supposed to have known better by now. You are no longer the freshman in college with an undeclared major who earned her PhD in life experience by giving her virginity to a young man who had given his away years before knowing that you existed. You are now a celebrated author and speaker specializing in the very thing that with "him," you still seem to battle: self-esteem, self-respect, self-control.

Yeah, Baby Girl, I know what you are about to say. All is fair in love and war, right? The thing is, when it comes to "him," I'm not so sure if you've ever known the difference between the two. Just think about it. Whenever you were with "him," did you feel protected (love) or exposed (war)? Did he meet your needs (love) or take whatever he could get (war)? Did he celebrate you (love) or harm you (war)? Did you trust him to stay (love) or fear he would leave (war)? Was he your lover (love) or sparring partner (war)?

– – – – – – – – – –

Now tell me, Baby Girl, ten years later, when it comes to these questions, what answers have really changed? Looks to me like you are still nursing wounds, healing scars, resetting a heart that has been broken in the same place twice. The only difference is that this time, it's going to take that much longer to heal.

I hate to say it, but your gut, your conscience, *I* told you not to let him in. You are simply too beautiful, too exceptional, too worthy for that now. But as a lover of music and movies, sometimes you get carried away by getting caught up in the hype of it all. To be honest, that's something that I love and even envy about you—your love for love. But not with "him." Not again. Not now and in this way. Not because he's not a "good guy," but because he's simply not good enough. You've come too far and he, in many ways, is right where you left him two *and* ten years ago.

I know that doesn't change the fact that your stomach is full of butterflies and your heart is beating faster with every passing moment leading up to Saturday. Even with "first love," "first abortion," "first heartbreak," and miles of secrets and memories between you—because he either never had the money or made the time (*ironically* and *surprisingly*)—there is still a "first time" left to be shared: you seeing him in a tux. Baby Girl, I never said he wasn't fine. But you can admire fine from afar.

But he is not the point. What I'm really writing to say is that you have nothing to be nervous about. I know you think fate must be playing a cruel joke to invite you to the one and probably only wedding where the two of you will be in attendance, but Baby Girl, this is a date with destiny. You need to go to this wedding and mourn and then bury your fantasy of being his wife. You need to go down the aisle walking first toward him and then turning away to your seat. It's symbolic of the direction your life will be taking now. And, as much as you are worrying about how he will look in a suit, you need to take pity on how he will feel when he sees your voluptuous silhouette in your vintage gown, silver heels, and butterfly jewelry. One thing he has been consistent about is telling you how beautiful you are and he's right.

This time, though, after all has been said and done, he will experience yet another "first."

This time, ironically and surprisingly, he will get something he needs so desperately from you whether either one of you realizes it or not. He *needs* to see what love—true, pure, committed love—looks like just one more time before you both part ways, not out of spite, but so he can have a standard for when he makes the attempt at real love again. Something that is hard to come by, just like you, Baby Girl.

So, get out your grape sorbet nail polish and lip gloss with that hint of plum sheen. It's no coincidence that, while his cousin will be in black and his wife will be in white, you will be in shades of purple—the color of royalty.

It's their wedding, "his" birthday, but Baby Girl, it's *your* graduation. You all have crossed the finish line. The race is over. And you, too, have won.

I love you.

© Shellie R. Warren, 2008

Freedom

Breaking the Cycle of Sexual Drama

As a dog returns to his own vomit, so a fool repeats his folly.

Proverbs 26:11 NKJV

Women might be able to fake orgasms. But men can fake a whole relationship.

Sharon Stone, actress

This book? I needed *a lot* of prayer to start . . . and complete it. I'm sure by now you can understand why. To sit down and write so much about a powerful issue . . . whew! It can take a lot out of a sistah! One of my closest friends told me about halfway in she had this vision of a tree falling when it came to the completion of this book. Not a tree in her life's yard. It was a tree in mine.

It seemed kind of odd and abstract, so we explored it a bit. We came to the conclusion that it probably symbolized a seed that had grown to the size of a tree in my life; how it was probably something that was deeply rooted in my spirit and needed to come up and out so that something better could fill it. Well, Marcella, my friend, here we are. My mother calls me a "stars and wonders" child, and so I'm sure it's no coincidence that chapter 7, the number that symbolizes completeness and perfection in the Bible, would be focusing on sexual drama cycles.

Anyone who knows me knows I'm a no-draft, let's-just-wing-it-with-the-Spirit kind of writer, and so everything you have read thus far has been what I believe God has directed me to say (with a hint of my personality, of course!). But this chapter? I'm sure by the time I am done, I will be in tears because I can already sense that it's about to free me of some things—once and for all! Revelations will be coming to us both—to me as I write this, to you as you read it. That's your heads-up. I'm not sure where we will end up exactly, so sit tight!

The Enemy will use what's worked before, until it doesn't work anymore.

If you didn't read the letter that I wrote to myself in the intro to this chapter, I ask you to do so before proceeding because it will help make some sense out of what I am about to say. You see, something I have learned about the Enemy and his tactics is that he will use what's worked before, until it doesn't work anymore. For me, that was my first love, the guy who was cast as the leading man in that letter.

God's Best

I can't believe how much power I gave him . . . for almost fifteen years of my life. Well, I take that back. Yes, I can. On certain levels, that is what sex is supposed to do. Especially sex with someone that you really care about.

I called him "David" in my first book, and while I don't think he'll mind my using his real name, because that name is bearing some other significance to me in this season, I will still refer to him as David in this book too. Partially because, in many ways, I think he has the spirit of the biblical David— sexual issues times ten and a lot of pride—but deep down a really good heart in search of some direction . . . *that only God can give.*

And while I'm here, let me say this, ladies: when you are a single woman in love with a single man, please don't take on the role of wife until you are his wife. Looking back, there were so many times when I wanted to take on responsibilities for his life that were not mine to take. We were "one" from the consequences of sexual sin but we did not have God's blessing to live as a married couple. His life was not and is not my responsibility. When you find yourself bonding to someone on a deeper level than friendship, you can be tempted to invest more in the relationship than you should. Don't.

Looking back, this is part of what messed me up. For as long as he's been in my life, in some shape, form, or fashion, I have wanted to give him something only God can give. I figured if I loved him enough, gave to him enough, even prayed for him enough, he would change. *Change is a choice* and at least last time I spoke with him, it wasn't one he really wanted to make. It took a minute, but now I love him enough to respect that. And I finally love me enough to move out of his way. I do continue to pray for him, though, because strange things happen when you choose not to change, not when it comes to us but his relationship with his Creator. I've been there, and even at this very moment, I continue to want the best for him.

How can I feel that way? Well, a miraculous thing happens when you start seeing who God wants you to be. You stop playing the martyr and you start living as the victor. As a matter of fact, if anyone was to blame for my pain, ultimately, at the end of the day, I'm sure it was me. In all honesty I sent myself through my drama cycle with him longer than I ever should have partially because *I chose not to change*. I chose not to pray, "Lord, if this is not your will, please remove this cup from me." Instead, my prayers went more like, "God, this is who I want and I don't care what you think about it, just bless me with him." Praise God for grace and mercy and yet, it's just in the past six months or so I am seeing God's no to David and a yes to something better. Not that he's bad, but I know he's not God's best for me—and quite possibly, I am not God's best for him. The Message version of Philippians 1:9–11 says:

> So this is my prayer: that your love will flourish and that you will not only love much but well. Learn to love appropriately. *You need to use your head and test your feelings so that your love is sincere and intelligent, not sentimental gush.* Live a lover's life, circumspect and exemplary, a life Jesus will be proud of: bountiful in fruits from the soul, making Jesus Christ attractive to all, getting everyone involved in the glory and praise of God.

Love can be romantic, but it's also, even in the eyes of God, a very practical thing. Ladies, when it comes to matters of the heart not working out in the way we would like, I wonder how many of us, while telling God how good a woman we are and how stupid a man he is for not seeing it, actually take a moment to stop and humble ourselves and say, "Well, wait a minute. God, if I am not the best woman *for him*, please let me be at peace with your decision to either change me or remove me. I love him enough to let him get to the woman you have in mind for his life, just as I want to get to the man you desire for me as well."

For years, because I had let David into my most holy place when it came to my mind, body, and spirit, I had conjured the fantasy that we would reunite and be married and live happily ever after. What I didn't want to face was that there were so many cracks in our foundation that it would take a real act (and approval) of God and a total surrender of both of us, on levels even I don't think I truly wanted to make, for that to happen.

When we met, he was fifteen and I was eighteen (an issue in itself). Fourteen years later, when he reached out to me *only* to apologize for the pain he had caused in our past (he found me after my book was released), he was a felon, a father of three, and even more wounded than when I first met him. As for me, I was broken, a mother of four aborted children (with one of them definitely being his and another a toss-up between him and another guy), and even more wounded than when he first met me. Where were we going to go with that? At the time, I saw no real concrete answers, but in fairness (to him), I think he understood that better than I ever did.

One of the best ways to avoid a drama cycle is to listen to what a man says and not what you want to hear.

So let me pause right here with some words of wisdom. One of the best ways to avoid a drama cycle with a man is to listen to what he says and not what you want to hear. When David emailed me, all he said was that he loved me, he was sorry for the pain he caused, and he hoped I was well. I heard, "I love you and I want us to be together so that I can fix all of the pain that I caused." Have mercy. Really?

From that moment on it was a roller-coaster ride like no other. We went to lunch and got emotional, exchanged phone numbers, and started keeping in touch. That transitioned into finding ways to make time to see one another, usually at a local Starbucks, but one time at his apartment, where we watched *The Notebook* (why did I bring *that* movie?) in a candlelit room. The movie was followed by a "who knows how long it lasted?" kissing fest that ended in his actually picking me up and putting me out of his apartment. Now remember, this was after *Inside of Me*, after I wrote 150–plus pages on why having premarital sex is not a good idea. I didn't care, though. This was my forbidden fruit of choice, and I was willing to risk whatever to have a bite.

A low sense of self-worth can really do a number on a girl. The next day, when I asked him why he didn't want to be intimate with me, he said, "I can't handle being intimate with you nor can I give you what you deserve." Some months later, when I tried again, he said, "Until I can be sure that you are the last person I will kiss, I will not kiss you again." The unhealthy side of Shellie took that to be rejection, but in healthy hindsight it's probably the most loving thing a man has ever done. He knew he could have taken full advantage of the situation but he chose not to. Love is indeed a choice. On that end he was much more of a safe place than I was or gave him credit for being.

Just a couple of days ago, I was interviewing a newly engaged couple (shout-out to Ahmad and Kim). The wife-to-be is a virgin; her husband-to-be is not but is committed to abstinence until they are married. When I asked him what made him commit to a lifestyle of abstinence *now*, he said, "In the past I *tolerated* relationships for the pleasure of sex. Men are always talking about wanting respect, but you must know what God wants from you and for your body. You must remember self-respect before expecting respect." It may not be talked about but, ladies, men are watching us beyond how we look. We actually hold a lot of influence with our words and actions. The Word even speaks to the fact that many unbelieving husbands can be won over to Christ by watching their wives' example (1 Peter 3:1–2). Ahmad's statement is wonderful testament that when you honor God, the right man will honor you because of it.

Good, Bad, or Indifferent

Refusing what's not good for you and having the ability to use foresight in making good choices, these are both great examples of self-respect. If you want a man to respect you, you must honor yourself enough by not compromising what you know you deserve, and what you deserve is what God says you deserve in his Word. As it relates to this book, that would be a husband, if sex and holistic intimacy are what you desire.

Yes, I think the reality is that not nearly enough of us know what we deserve. Our fathers may not have been there to show us. Our mothers may have been too jaded to tell us. Classmates may have been too catty to affirm us. And Lord knows Hollywood is too superficial to guide us. But the Bible says that, like David, we should praise God because we are fearfully and wonderfully made. All of God's works are marvelous, and he knows our souls very well (Ps. 139:14–16). This also means that God knows what's good for us and what's not. He knows *who's* good for us and who's not and when they are good for us and when they are not. He knows what we deserve; he knows this very well.

As it related to David and me—as it relates to any man and me—one thing that is not good for my soul is having a man who does not serve the Lord. Ironically, for me, that was always my head trip, though. I just wasn't attracted to "saved" men. I always wanted to "fix one up." And you know what? I have come to realize *even that* was symptomatic of my low self-worth. *I didn't think I deserved a man who had it all together.* I had to get one who was a project. I'm sure a part of it was because, growing up, that is what my mother and her marriage looked like: a woman with a broken man she had to fix (parents, please watch the example that you set for your children). Another part of it was that I felt so bad about myself that "working my magic," whether in or out of the bedroom, made me feel as though I were really doing something, that I was actually worth something. A healthy man would be able to call me on my crap. A sick man would either be mesmerized by or fearful of refusing what I had to offer—good, bad, or indifferent.

Good, bad, or indifferent. All of the people who have heard me speak on this topic know I have a weakness for thugs. My mom says it's because my daddy is a thug (check), and I speculate that a big part of it is because my first was a thug (check, check). But very recently, God told me to check out the definition of that word as well: "a cruel or vicious ruffian, robber, or murderer; a cutthroat; a hoodlum."

Whoa! Checkmate. Look at what I was speaking into my existence. Now, every guy in my life wasn't a thug in the classic sense. Most of them have college degrees with no police record. But when I think about *the character* of most of those bad boys, *cruel* and *cutthroat* would fit the bill for over 90 percent of them. But here's the thing: I brought those relationships on myself! Even in spite of all of the blood, sweat, and tears I experienced, especially with David, I now have to accept I wasn't the victim of anything. It was the lack of respect for the power of my own choices that got me into those emotionally draining situations.

The title of this chapter is "Freedom: Breaking the Cycle of Sexual Drama." Freedom happens not through external factors but internal resolves. Just this week I was watching a show about a woman who keeps having to deal with the fact that her husband is in love with his first love, who was another woman who came before her. She said something to her husband, but I felt she said it directly to me: "I love you, but I don't live in the past. I can't even relate to what you are going through . . . tell me what that is like."

Listen to me: if you are currently in love with *the memory* of something, please let it go, for your sake and the sake of the person who is still bound to the way that things used to be in your head. Was it not in the 1997 urban classic film *Love Jones* that Nia Long's character said to her ex-fiancé, "All we have are all these years"? In no way did she live in the *past* that had *passed*.

Sometimes we find ourselves holding on to the amount of time we shared with a person, as though that were reason enough to stay together. If, however, we were asked to give more reasons to stay, we wouldn't be able to come up with a single one. We stay because we are afraid of starting over.

The Bible says, "Therefore, if anyone is in Christ, he is a new creation; old things have passed away; behold, all things have become new" (2 Cor. 5:17 NKJV). I don't know about you, but that reads to me like being in Christ and releasing old things is a day-by-day process. Every day we make the choice to be in Christ and every day we have to let old things pass away. We have to allow God to renew in us what he will. It took a real "Come to Jesus" meeting for me to accept that I had a hard time getting free from sexual sin, in part, because I continued to stay around men who had no interest in sexual purity. Back then, I didn't really think about it.

We stay because we are afraid of starting over.

Now that I am coming to understand more about the power of divine purpose and the Enemy's agenda to destroy it, I see those men were in my space to keep me from doing what I know God has created me to do: help people on the path to sexual wholeness and restoration. Because those men were not living in the will of God, especially as it related to God's purpose for sex, they were not a part of God's perfect will for my life. I have learned, the oh-so-very-hard way, that what God wants to grant us doesn't bring with it lots of baggage and drama; that if I want it—whatever "it" may be—and I don't have it, either it's not the right time . . . or in my best interest.

Do you know where your fights and arguments come from? They come from the selfish desires that war within you. You want things, but you do not have them. So you are ready to kill and are jealous of other people, but you still cannot get what you want. So you argue and fight. You do not get what you want, because you do not ask God. Or when you ask, you do not receive because the reason you ask is wrong. *You want things so you can use them for your own pleasures.*

James 4:1–3

With confession comes healing, right (James 5:16)? As it relates to this particular subject, I can't remember praying for the souls of those men or that they would become what God wanted them to be *for their own sake* and that I would be made into a suitable helpmate for them. Heck no! If I prayed at all, my prayers were always "Give him to me"; "Don't let her take him from me"; "Why doesn't he love me like I love him? Make him!" Those desperate requests and spoiled-brat demands went totally against God's Word. He clearly said I wouldn't have them because I wanted to use them for my own greed, my own lust, my own agenda. Wondering what God thought about it was an afterthought, usually after the relationship ended.

Praise God that all things do work together for the good of those who love him and are called according to his purpose (Rom. 8:28). I'm sure I could have provided you with content for this book without having a past that was so spiritually negligent or morally disobedient, but praise God he is redeeming my past. Trust me, going through this helps me understand why it's so hard to end such cycles, especially the ones that have sex attached to them.

The End of the Story

I'm sure some of the nosier gals (just kidding) are wondering what finally happened with David and me. Well, after spending so much of my energy on something that, for all intents and purposes, should have never started to begin with, I set a date last fall to meet with him so that we could once and for all figure out what we were doing with each other as it related to our lives. I had to speak that weekend in Seattle and I asked some women to pray that God's will would be done. I rushed off the plane and ran out to his side of town, to a local Starbucks, and waited . . . and waited. I left messages on his phone and waited some more. He never showed, and I haven't heard from him since, other than an email on his birthday (in January) to say that he would always love me (he must have been listening to Dolly Parton or Whitney Houston that day), and another recent email from him, one that I quickly deleted. I have been around the tree long enough to know when the serpent is ready to try to trick me . . . again.

How did he handle it, "it" being my heart? As a cruel and cutthroat man—all the things I loved in a man—that's how he handled my heart. And I invited all of it into my life. First Corinthians 13:4 says that love is patient. Hmph. It's a sobering reality how patient I was, to the point of personal stagnation, with a man who was hurting me. Whether it was intentional or rooted in his moral ignorance of how to treat a woman, I still took it and came back for more. A part of it was because he was my first, and sex is powerful. Another part was because I hadn't forgiven myself (or him) for giving him something so precious. I couldn't move on with my life.

Let me address the man himself. David, if you're reading this (and I pray that you are so that you can save a copy for your beautiful daughters; then perhaps they won't have to live out our testimony), this is for you: You haven't had my body in years, but there is a part of you that has always had a part of my mind and spirit. I love you and I am so sorry for not being God's will in your life. Please forgive me. I am ready now to really move on to what God wants for me. I pray that you remain open to what God has for you. You deserve to see how good his plans are and how great your life can be if you would just surrender to them.

Ladies, that is the way to break a drama cycle.

We stay in harmful cycles when we keep returning to something we never should have had in the first place (if you have to go against the Word or come out of your femininity to get it, that's your cue) and when we refuse to walk the faith line. It's impossible to limit God to being one or even a hundred things, but I can assure you that if there's one adjective you can be sure of, when it comes to our Father, it's *gracious*.

He is all about moving into new seasons (Ecclesiastes 3); he's all about pouring new wine into new wineskins (Matt. 9:16–17).

Marcella, I get your dream now. You were by my side when my relationship with David started and you are still by my side. That's love. David was the tree—what he represented in my life. You see, what I haven't told you (yet) is that God showed me this week that he was going to uproot one tree and replace it with another, not a seed but another full-grown tree. Not the tree of the knowledge of good and evil . . . but the tree of life.

Living Out the Answer

I beg you . . . to have patience with everything unresolved in your heart and try to love the questions themselves as if they were locked rooms or books written in a very foreign language. Don't search for the answers, which could not be given now, because you would not be able to live them. And the point is, to live everything now. Perhaps then, someday far in the future, you will gradually, without even noticing it, live your way into the answer.

Rainer Maria Rilke, German poet

- - - - - - - - - -

8

Identity

Finding (Godly) Femininity

A capable, intelligent, and virtuous woman—who is he who can find her? She is far more precious than jewels and her value is far above rubies or pearls.

Proverbs 31:10 AMP

A woman who is not feminine is a monster in creation.

Elizabeth Missing Sewell, English novelist

While the majority of this book has addressed the issue of sexual immorality, as we near the end, we will be talking about it less and less. Don't get me wrong; I'm sure many of you picked up this book to learn about sexual brokenness and how to be made whole from it, but when it comes to healing from sexual misuse, from personal experience, I've come to see that it's the soul more than the body that needs to be tended.

- -

Let me give you a biblical example of what a woman lacking femininity vs. a woman who is full of femininity can do—to herself, to her man, and to society as a whole. Then we will modernize this issue. The book of Esther tells us (mainly) about two beautiful women, two queens and how their choices affected both them and those around them. The first lovely lady was Queen Vashti. When the Bible makes it a point to mention that a woman was beautiful, to me that means she really must've been something for the eyes to behold. When it comes to physical beauty, Queen Vashti definitely held her own. Esther 1 paints the picture of a huge banquet that King Xerxes had in his kingdom. Queen Vashti also gave a banquet for the women in the royal palace of King Xerxes. Here is the story:

> On the seventh day of the banquet, King Xerxes was very happy, because he had been drinking much wine. He gave a command to the seven eunuchs who served him—Mehuman, Biztha, Harbona, Bigtha, Abagtha, Zethar, and Carcas. He commanded them to bring him Queen Vashti, wearing her royal crown. She was to come to show her beauty to the people and important men, because she was very beautiful. *The eunuchs told Queen Vashti about the king's command, but she refused to come.* Then the king became very angry; his anger was like a burning fire.
>
> It was a custom for the king to ask advice from experts about law and order. So King Xerxes spoke with the wise men who would know the right thing to do. The wise men the king usually talked to were Carshena, Shethar, Admatha, Tarshish, Meres, Marsena, and Memucan, seven of the important men of Persia and Media. These seven had special privileges to see the king and had the highest rank in the kingdom. The king asked them, "What does the law say must be done to Queen Vashti? She has not obeyed the command of King Xerxes, which the eunuchs took to her."
>
> Then Memucan said to the king and the other important men, "Queen Vashti has not done wrong to the king alone.

She has also done wrong to all the important men and all the people in all the empire of King Xerxes. All the wives of the important men of Persia and Media will hear about the queen's actions. Then they will no longer honor their husbands. They will say, 'King Xerxes commanded Queen Vashti to be brought to him, but she refused to come.' Today the wives of the important men of Persia and Media have heard about the queen's actions. So they will speak in the same way to their husbands, and there will be no end to disrespect and anger.

"So, our king, if it pleases you, give a royal order, and let it be written in the laws of Persia and Media, which cannot be changed. The law should say Vashti is never again to enter the presence of King Xerxes. Also let the king give her place as queen to someone who is better than she is. And let the king's order be announced everywhere in his enormous kingdom. Then all the women will respect their husbands, from the greatest to the least."

Esther 1:10–20

The message is clear: when it comes to Queen Vashti, no matter how beautiful she was on the outside, her attitude was foul. Her blatant disrespect of not only her position but herself angered the king and his advisors because she had been elevated to a place of great influence. Women were watching her every move. What she did, other women would soon imitate.

What you do (or don't do) can take you a long way.

Ladies, even now, *even if you are single*, someone is watching you. Someone is watching what you say, how you say it, when you say it, and why; someone is also watching how your actions reflect your words. What you do (or don't do) can take you a long way—a long way good or a long way not so good.

When Queen Vashti's attitude got her demoted, a new queen had to be selected. Most of us are familiar with this part of the story, so here are the main verses that I encourage you to meditate on:

> When the king's command and order had been heard, many girls had been brought to the palace in Susa and put under the care of Hegai. Esther was also taken to the king's palace and put under the care of Hegai, who was in charge of the women. *Esther pleased Hegai, and he liked her. So Hegai quickly began giving Esther her beauty treatments and special food. He gave her seven servant girls chosen from the king's palace. Then he moved her and her seven servant girls to the best part of the women's quarters.*
>
> *Esther did not tell anyone about her family or who her people were, because Mordecai had told her not to.* Every day Mordecai walked back and forth near the courtyard where the king's women lived to find out how Esther was and what was happening to her.
>
> Before a girl could take her turn with King Xerxes, she had to complete twelve months of beauty treatments that were ordered for the women. For six months she was treated with oil and myrrh and for six months with perfumes and cosmetics. Then she was ready to go to the king. Anything she asked for was given to her to take with her from the women's quarters to the king's palace. *In the evening she would go to the king's palace, and in the morning she would return to another part of the women's quarters. There she would be placed under the care of Shaashgaz, the king's eunuch in charge of the slave women. The girl would not go back to the king again unless he was pleased with her and asked for her by name.*

> Esther 2:8–14

You do see the line that says she went to the king's palace in the evening and returned in the morning, right? Has anyone seen one of the 80 billion seasons of *The Bachelor*? When a girl went to his room for the night . . . it's pretty easy to assume what happened. Therefore, I'm not using this story as a biblical example of abstinence, but it is a wonderful story of femininity. There was something about Esther's character that caught Hegai's attention; she found favor and was moved to the next round: pampered treatment.

Ladies, when you are sweet and gracious—two things Esther was with the king once she became queen—you'll be amazed how far it will take you. In King Xerxes' palace, people saw women—lots of women—all of the time. I'm certain Esther had a beauty that caused men to take a second look, but it was *her character* that made them want to go from looks to discussion, from discussion to pursuit.

The story goes on to say that after twelve months of treatments, she was ready for the king. In the evening she would go and in the morning she would return . . . not to go back to the king again *unless he called her by name.* Let me tell you, as a control-freak-in-recovery, how hard this one is for me at times. One of my older women mentors used to tell me that if a guy wants to talk to you, he'll call. Wisdom often trumps reasoning. So, loud and clear: Honey, *if a guy wants to talk to you, he'll call.*

Another trait of Esther—one that bears going before the Father and asking him to give you—is she was confident in who she was; she knew she had something that was undeniable. She didn't have to convince the king of that. She just had to be Esther. In time, if you read the rest of the story, you will see that she was . . . and then some.

Now this is something to keep in mind as you read the rest of this chapter: many of us have a Queen Vashti rather than a Queen Esther spirit. This chapter is going to help you bury the former and resurrect the latter. God didn't just make you a female. He made you a woman—someone who is supposed to be feminine.

When it comes to finding (or fine-tuning) your femininity, let me start out this chapter by saying that, if you don't have some male friends—and by this, I mean males whom you don't have any kind of sexual history or current sexual tension with—please get some. Now, I may be bucking the traditional system a bit (more) in saying this, but most of this book is based on lessons I have learned. One thing I've learned is that in my pursuit of abstinence, staying away from men totally only makes matters worse. No matter what your current resolve is about men, whether you love 'em, lust 'em, or hate their guts, we all need them in our lives.

Daddy . . .

Ladies, no matter what you may think about your earthly/ biological father, the truth (and please let the truth set you free—John 8:32) is that *none of us* would exist without them. You may not respect what your father has done (or not done) but do make it a point to honor (Exod. 20:12) the vessel that got you here. Whether you are (physically) the spitting image of him, or the only thing that you seem to have in common is your last name (if that), every time you look in the mirror, a part of that man is staring right back at you . . . *and that's okay.* That's what DNA is all about!

Some of us are unhappy with a part of who we are because we are so mad at who helped to make us who we are. The Bible commissions us to love our neighbors as ourselves (Gal. 5:14). It also tells us that we owe no one anything other than to love him or her (Rom. 13:8). Now if you want to Facebook me to tell me what your translation says, feel free. Do know, though, that I go to BibleGateway.com pretty often to cross-reference Scriptures, and I have yet to come across one that says, "Love your neighbor unless it's your absentee dad" or "You owe everyone love except your triflin' father." Growing as a godly, feminine woman in Christ includes loving your daddy, no matter the form his sinful nature takes.

When I was working out some issues with my own father and stepfather, I went to 1 Corinthians 13, the Love Chapter. At the time I was trying to restore some kind of emotional equilibrium in my life regarding these men, and it seemed patience, kindness, and not being rude were the things I struggled with most. Again, I am speaking from personal experience, but since this chapter is about getting our godly femininity (back), let me just say that unresolved anger usually leads to bitterness. In turn, bitterness battles with beauty—feminine beauty—in ways you've probably never imagined. You know by now that I like to define words, so here's the meaning of *bitter:* hard to bear, grievous, distressful, causing pain, piercing, stinging, characterized by intense antagonism or hostility, resentful, or cynical. None of these sound very beautiful, do they?

Growing as a godly, feminine woman in Christ includes loving your daddy.

Proverbs 5:3–5 (NKJV) says, "For the lips of an immoral woman drip honey, and her mouth is smoother than oil; but in the end she is *bitter* as wormwood, sharp as a two-edged sword. Her feet go down to death, her steps lay hold of hell."

Ephesians 4:30–32 says:

And do not make the Holy Spirit sad. The Spirit is God's proof that you belong to him. God gave you the Spirit to show that God will make you free when the final day comes. Do not be *bitter* or angry or mad. Never shout angrily or say things to hurt others. Never do anything evil. Be kind and loving to each other, and forgive each other just as God forgave you in Christ.

James 3:13–15 says:

Are there those among you who are truly wise and understanding? Then they should show it by living right and doing good things with a gentleness that comes from wisdom. But if you are selfish and have *bitter* jealousy in your hearts, do not brag. Your bragging is a lie that hides the truth. That kind of "wisdom" does not come from God but from the world. It is not spiritual; it is from the devil.

And the main passage I want to focus on for this chapter is Hebrews 12:14–16 (NKJV):

> Pursue peace with all people, and holiness, without which no one will see the Lord: looking carefully lest anyone fall short of the grace of God; lest any root of *bitterness* springing up cause trouble, and by this many become defiled; lest there be any fornicator or profane person like Esau, who for one morsel of food sold his birthright.

Did you catch it? Did you read one result of how bitterness can manifest itself? Bitterness, an emotion that can be defined as "hard to bear, grievous, distressful," is your enemy and, once again, if you are not careful, it can attack even your approach to sexuality. This Scripture says that bitterness causes trouble, it defiles many, *and* it can lead one to becoming a fornicator or profane. Bottom line? Nothing good comes from it, so please, don't be bitter.

No matter what, determine not to give any person the power to impair the quality of your life. And that's what a person for whom you feel bitterness does! Before anything, *you are God's daughter*, and you are precious in his sight. This chapter is about living out one of our most unique and necessary traits: femininity. If you want to have your femininity restored, a good place to start is by making it a point to forgive (Mark 11:25) and love (be patient with, be kind to, be not rude toward) your father, not just for his sake but for yours.

When it comes to the kind of restoration that God has led me to address in this chapter, because the world has jacked up so many ways that we see ourselves, I guess it would help to define feminine, first by the dictionary's terms and then by the Word.

She's a Lady

The dictionary definition of *feminine*: pertaining to a woman or girl; having qualities traditionally ascribed to women, as sensitivity or gentleness. Feminine women are sensitive and gentle. Why fight against your physical birthright? Your spiritual inheritance? Why settle for being less than what Titus 2 advises you to be? Because, although these verses speak to married women specifically, I am a firm believer that when Proverbs 18:22 says, "he who finds a wife finds a good thing," even a single woman must have wifely qualities so that she can be "found."

> In the same way, teach older women to be holy in their behavior, not speaking against others or enslaved to too much wine, but teaching what is good. Then they can teach the young women to love their husbands, to love their children, to be wise and pure, to be good workers at home, to be kind, and to yield to their husbands. Then no one will be able to criticize the teaching God gave us.
>
> Titus 2:3–5

The qualities of femininity? We, as women, should have a spiritually pure quality—we should not be gossips or drunks (ain't nothin' worse than seeing a drunk woman!). We are to teach what is beneficial. We are to love our husband and children; we are to be wise and pure; we are to be homemakers who are kind and submissive to our husband.

Before some of you buck up, remember that while the world may not operate under this system, God is not threatened or moved to change by that fact. I have mentioned several times throughout this book that the wisdom of the world is foolishness to God (1 Cor. 3:18–19), and the Bible also tells us that, when we seek the kingdom of heaven and his righteousness *first*, often the things we try unsuccessfully to get on our own are given to us (Matt. 6:33).

It was "Tough Love 101" (Heb. 12:6) through which I came to accept that certain things about me were not feminine, no matter how much of an "hourglass" I was perceived to be. I would gossip with the best of 'em and I definitely had a season when my life was anything but pure. As we've seen throughout this book, that is just how the Enemy wants us to be: *out of God's purpose*. Do you remember back in the Garden when God said he would put enmity (a feeling or condition of hostility, hatred, ill will, animosity, antagonism) between Eve and Satan *and* between Satan and Eve's descendants? When it comes to our femininity, the Enemy is out to steal, kill, and destroy (John 10:10) in any and every way he can.

If there is a housewife reading this book, don't let the pressures of Corporate America steal the gift, privilege, and pleasure of being a housewife. According to God's Word, this is the epitome of femininity, and so of course the Enemy would want to take that peace of mind away from you. Greater is he who is in you, right (1 John 4:4)?

Sexy . . . or Not?

There is another biblical side to the feminine coin—what happens when it is not fully developed. One thing that seems to be a real issue is that a lot of focus is put on how a woman *looks* rather than *who* she is. Her body more than her character. I remember the first time I read the following verses in 2 Timothy and *how silly I felt* because I realized that I put my emphasis on the wrong thing. That's because I didn't guard my heart (Prov. 4:23), and many men were able to take advantage of my ignorance about my self-worth.

> For people will be lovers of self and [utterly] self-centered, lovers of money and aroused by an inordinate [greedy] desire for wealth, proud and arrogant and contemptuous boasters.

They will be abusive (blasphemous, scoffing), disobedient to parents, ungrateful, unholy and profane.

[They will be] without natural [human] affection (callous and inhuman), relentless (admitting of no truce or appeasement); [they will be] slanderers (false accusers, troublemakers), intemperate and loose in morals and conduct, uncontrolled and fierce, haters of good.

[They will be] treacherous [betrayers], rash, [and] inflated with self-conceit. [They will be] lovers of sensual pleasures and vain amusements more than and rather than lovers of God.

For [although] they hold a form of piety (true religion), they deny and reject and are strangers to the power of it [their conduct belies the genuineness of their profession]. Avoid [all] such people [turn away from them].

For among them are those who worm their way into homes and captivate silly and weak-natured and spiritually dwarfed women, loaded down with [the burden of their] sins [and easily] swayed and led away by various evil desires and seductive impulses.

[These weak women will listen to anybody who will teach them]; they are forever inquiring and getting information, but are never able to arrive at a recognition and knowledge of the Truth.

2 Timothy 3:2–7 AMP

I don't care how tight your dress is, how sexy your lips are, how many men pass out when you walk by. Proverbs 31:10 (NKJV) tells us that "Charm is deceitful and beauty is passing, but a woman who fears the LORD, she shall be praised." Did you really catch that? It's *a woman who honors God* who will receive praise (approval, admiration, commendation), at least the kind of praise that is of value (whistles from men *don't count!*).

The Message version of Luke 6:25–26 says that our mission is to live what's true not what's popular, and this may challenge you just a bit. The Word clearly tells us what kind of woman should be praised, but as you flip through the television channels, you see the kind of women who *are* being praised. And more times than not, their character is not the focus. If they have lips, hips, and fingertips (and often a pair of fake breasts and a long weave as well), then that seems to be all they really need to be admired, according to society's standards.

However, when it comes to being the kind of woman who catches God's eye and favor, nowhere in the Bible—trust me, I've looked—is a woman praised for being what the world seems to love, well, lust, so much. Nowhere is a woman in the Bible praised for being sexy. *Nowhere!*

> A *woman who fears the* Lord, *she shall be praised.*

I definitely think that sexiness has its time and place. I mean, I would certainly hope that my future husband would find me sexually interesting and exciting; who wouldn't? Deeper yet, who shouldn't? But as someone who has been told for most of my life that I am sexy, that's kind of the point that I'm trying to make: I will be the first to raise my hand and say that I had, and on some levels still have, to be purged of wanting to be sexually desirable to men in general rather than to my husband specifically. What's the point or purpose of having a man look at me and want to have sex with me when he's not supposed to have sex with me? And if I, as a woman, was put on the earth to be a helper, who is that helping? What's wise and pure (the very definitions of femininity) about being a temptress, morally deplorable, instead of a supporter of what's godly?

Just yesterday I was talking to one of my girlfriends who is physically attractive: long hair, flawless skin, a great shape. Indeed, like her namesake in the Bible, Rachel is something to behold. The interesting thing is that when she was single (and a virgin), "extremely cute" or "pretty" seemed like the best way to describe her. When she got back from her honeymoon, while I couldn't initially put my finger on it, something was different. Becoming a wife—and a sexually active woman—had matured her, seemingly overnight. Her sexiness is something special. To this day, some six years later, she and I discuss how cautious she needs to be in how men react to her now that she is having sex *even within covenant*; however, it's not something she should apologize for. *She's having sex with her husband*, as she is supposed to. What you do is a reflection of who you are. As we were sitting on her porch talking about how excited she was to be celebrating her upcoming anniversary with her husband, she said, "Do you know what he said to me once after we were married? That he was so glad he didn't see my nipples while we were dating. I mean not even through my clothing. He was grateful that I wore the right bras so that none of that was exposed . . . until it was time for them to be . . . until we were married."

You may think that is a very old-fashioned and conservative way of thinking, but life lessons are teaching me that some traditions are meant to be kept. One of my favorite books of all time is *Real Christianity* by William Wilberforce, and one of his greatest points is that far too many Christ-followers are caught up in cultural Christianity rather than authentic faith. Culture changes all of the time, but Hebrews 13:8 tells us that Christ is the same yesterday, today, and forever. Do you know the really tripped-out thing about that verse in Scripture? Just four lines up is where it tells us that God will judge fornicators and adulterers. Yesterday he said that. Today he is saying that. He will forever feel that way. He will forever desire for us to be sexually whole people, to wait until marriage, and to be responsible with our sexuality, both in our presentation and in our actions, until the time when he returns (see Matt. 22:30).

That got me thinking about something one of my married male friends recently said to me. He was telling me about how his music studio's next-door neighbor has a "For Rent" sign up even though the space is already rented out. He said,

"Shellie, don't dress like you're 'for rent' when your space is occupied."

He was speaking of being cautious about my attire once I am married, but we all know the Bible says that even when we're not married, we are not our own; we are to glorify God with our body *and* our spirit (1 Cor. 6:19–20). The world says a woman uses what she has to get what she wants. The Word of God says that a woman honors her temple (her body) and, according to 2 Timothy, a woman who is led by sensual desires and impulses is considered silly and weak-natured. In spite of how the world may revere silly women, there is nothing feminine about them at all. That just addresses the physical side of things. Celebrated American feminist Gloria Steinem was once quoted as saying one of the most fitting and profound things on this subject: "Some of us are becoming the men we wanted to marry."

I don't know about you, but I had to let that one marinate within me for a couple of days. It rang true with me and I actually posted it on my Facebook page one day. It was funny to see the responses of women. Most of them said something along the lines of "Whoa" or "Crap," but there were some who almost wanted to defend the statement: "Well, when you've been single and doing it for yourself for as long as I have, you do get to a place where you become the man that you want."

I hear you. And my ears sting from the sound of wounds tinged with bitterness. That defense is about as dysfunctional as the single moms who say they are the mother and the father of their children. You are not, and will never be, both a man and a woman in a child's life. You may be doubling up on responsibilities because the father has gone spiritually and emotionally AWOL (financially, some of you still need to get him on child support), but no matter how many self-help books may insist, you cannot be a man . . . unless you are a man.

Being feminine is not something that automatically comes with being a bride or a wife. Whether married or single, you are still called to be a feminine woman. I've mentioned this Scripture before, and it's one of my absolute, all-time favorites about being a godly wife:

> In the same way, you wives should yield to your husbands. Then, if some husbands do not obey God's teaching, they will be persuaded to believe without anyone's saying a word to them. *They will be persuaded by the way their wives live. Your husbands will see the pure lives you live with your respect for God.* It is not fancy hair, gold jewelry, or fine clothes that should make you beautiful. No, your beauty should come from within you—*the beauty of a gentle and quiet spirit* that will never be destroyed and is very precious to God. In this same way the holy women who lived long ago and followed God made themselves beautiful, yielding to their own husbands. Sarah obeyed Abraham, her husband, and called him her master. *And you women are true children of Sarah if you always do what is right and are not afraid.*
>
> 1 Peter 3:3–6

Yes, this is a message written to wives. While you may not be one (yet), the Bible says that when a man finds *a wife,* he finds a good thing; not a man who finds a piece of eye candy, but a man who finds a woman with wifely characteristics—someone who is a wife before he even gets to her. Well, ladies, do you see all of the power that's housed within a woman who knows who God called her to be and is actually bold enough to buck the world's system in order to live it out? A godly woman can convict a man's heart to change just by his watching how she lives (if you've never read the book *Sacred Influence* by Gary Thomas, after reading this chapter, it would be time to invest in it!). A godly woman doesn't have to be flamboyant or loud in her appearance or her actions, because she knows that her gentle and quiet *spirit* is untouchable.

Okay, I'll pause here for just a moment. A loud voice? I most certainly have one, and if you do as well, celebrate it! God made us all just the way we are for a reason. But in my pursuit of godliness, I have noticed—and people have told me—that my energy, my presence, my spirit is much different than it used to be; now I am loud when necessary (and not as often as I thought it would be, either). A gentle spirit is a simple one that is kind, manageable, calm, and polite. A quiet spirit is one that is restrained in speech, tranquil, and peaceful. Is it me or do those words almost sound like a vacation at a spa resort? A woman whose spirit is gentle and kind is a pleasure to be around.

A woman whose spirit is gentle and kind is a pleasure to be around.

I remember once an ex-boyfriend of mine telling me that a woman should be a sanctuary for a man. Now your religious thinking may want to challenge that, but you know I'm a definitions girl and one definition of that word is "a sacred or holy place." Being that we are the temple of the Holy Spirit (1 Cor. 6:19), on many levels, a sanctuary is *exactly* how we should be seen and received!

The final point in these verses in 1 Peter that I wanted to bring up is the last line. It says that we are true daughters of Sarah if we always do what is right and are not afraid. Sadly, I know that being a feminine woman is often associated with being a weak one, but does this description in 1 Peter sound like a feeble or helpless person to you? I know a ton of men, strong and successful men (at least to the eye), who don't appear to do what's right, seemingly because they are afraid to do so. It takes amazing faith and an immovable, internal resolve to live each day in a way that is pleasing to God without being fearful of how the world may treat you as a result.

Again, just a few verses down from one assurance, we see another. First Peter 3:13–16 tells us:

> If you are trying hard to do good, no one can really hurt you. *But even if you suffer for doing right, you are blessed.* "Don't be afraid of what they fear; do not dread those things" [Isaiah

8:12–13]. But respect Christ as the holy Lord in your hearts. Always be ready to answer everyone who asks you to explain about the hope you have, but *answer in a gentle way and with respect.* Keep a clear conscience so that those who speak evil of your good life in Christ will be made ashamed.

It takes a strong person to be open to suffering just for doing what is right, and did you catch the other verse I put in italics? Answering someone in a gentle and respectful way isn't a "girly" thing; it's a godly thing. It's my personal belief that because we were created and ordained to help those around us, when we apply these instructions to our lives on a consistent basis, there is a supernaturalness that kicks in. Our gentleness, our kindness, our standing for what's right in spite of the potential outcome, our example to support and assist others in a way that only a woman, a godly woman, can.

You can probably say it with me now: God knows it. Satan knows it. It's certainly time that we know it.

A message on restoring our femininity is a book in itself (you might want to go to Amazon.com and check out *A Gentle and Quiet Spirit: Of Great Worth to God* by Virginia Lefler), but I hope this provided an introduction into why being truly feminine is so important to our daily lives. God is relying on the power of a woman, living the way he created her to be, to influence and positively alter the lives/hearts/souls of the men around her. Your looks may *attract* a man, but very rarely, if ever, do they evoke a heart change.

It's the latter that God is always after.

A Letter from God

- - - - - - - - - - -

My Daughter,

You are right where you are supposed to be. So many people have theories and insights on how couples are to come together and the truth is that many miss it by interpreting what they want rather than what I choose. A man pursuing, a girl refusing, these are not necessarily the optimal conditions for mate selection. Adam did not "pursue" the Woman, nor did she spend her time creating ways to make it challenging for him to do so. Just like one's purpose or date of birth and death, it is *I* who determines the "who, when, and where" of authentic and Spirit-led matrimony and intimacy. It is the responsibility of both parties to follow as I lead.

You are not waiting on some man to "get his act together" or "see you for who you really are," and no matter how it may appear to you in the physical realm, in the spiritual sense, "he" is right on schedule, *my schedule*. You are not to be listening to what man says, no matter in what form the voice may reveal itself (media, tradition, statistics, naysayers, and so on). Remember, I decided when it was time for Adam to receive the miracle of female assistance and so if you have an issue with physical time, don't take that up with anyone other than me; even then, know that I have your best interest at heart. Far too many of my daughters are consuming themselves with fear and anxiety about things that are really none of their concern. My ways are not your ways and until I unite you with the one you are purposed to benefit, his whereabouts and activities are not to be a priority to you. If you have not been joined to him yet, it's simply because it's not the right moment. He is not ready and neither are you. There are finishing touches that must be placed on you both and no matter how you may feel or what you might think, I am a God of order. I will not be pressured to move outside of my plan.

I know it must be hard. Flesh never likes to submit to my will. But please let me continue to mold you. Before you ever existed, you were hand-selected for someone and that has not changed. As the Creator, I am excited about my handiwork. Don't go looking for answers to questions you are not able to conceptualize or present in a way that will intimidate me to react or respond. As I did with your parents, let me have the pleasure of presenting you as a gift to your mate. Ask your mother and father if they will ever forget the first time they saw your face. I want "him" to experience a similar thrill. If you want to channel out your energies, get excited about how excited I am about you, about how blessed I know he will be to have you!

Again, don't concern yourself about the time. I am timeless. Concern yourself instead with remaining in my hands so that I can perfect you to be all that he needs, so that when it's the right moment, there will be no fear, no hesitation, no question that you are indeed the one whom he is meant to live out the rest of his days on the earth with. Far too many women are not praised on their wedding day by their husbands in the way I would've liked because they did not allow me the opportunity to complete them to be what was required, and the man was not discerning enough to know the true purpose that his companion was meant to serve in his life.

I want more for you. Love me enough to let me give it to you. Just as you are to be a blessing to him, he is to be provider and protector for you; he is to bless you as well in ways even your prayers have yet to articulate, but in my infinite wisdom, I know you deserve.

Remember, above all else that, like faith (Heb. 11:6), marriage is a spiritual union. This is the time to remove yourself from your senses, from what the physical is telling you, and tap into your spirit. This is when you can please me most by standing and believing that I am true to my Word, even when you don't see, feel, or hear evidence of its manifestation. The spirit always moves at what you all call "light years" ahead of the flesh. It takes it some time to catch up. Be patient (1 Cor. 13:4).

Stay in my will and I will show you the way—a way that leads to love, bliss, and happiness, a place where you will feel naked and not ashamed . . . until death parts you. A place where your future husband will restfully await you.

I love you. Be still and know. *Really know.* I do.

Your Heavenly Father

9

Perseverance

Patience with the Process

Love is patient.

1 Corinthians 13:4

Patience is bitter, but its fruit is sweet.

Ancient proverb

Love is patient. *Love is patient.*

Currently I am walking out a journey with a friend who is showing me this in a way that I have never experienced before. It's one thing to *say* you will be patient with someone. It's something else entirely to try to actually *follow through*. When you are patient, you are "bearing provocation, annoyance, misfortune, delay, hardship, pain, and so on with fortitude and calm and without complaint, anger, or the like," and you are "quietly and steadily persevering or diligent, especially in detail or exactness." It takes a real act of faith in anyone's life to do that!

I am led to believe that if you have gotten this far in the book, some things are breaking, if not broken, in you. You want to do better but you may not be completely sure how. Sister, I've been there. When I first started this abstinence journey, I had no idea what I was in for or how I would find the strength to say I went eleven months, let alone a couple of years, but love is patient, God is love (1 John 4:16) and God loves me (John 3:16).

God knows what he's doing . . . even if you don't.

When I wrote down what I heard God saying to me in the letter that begins this chapter, I was moved. I was really moved, actually, because it spoke to my situation on so many levels. For me, when it comes to this abstinence/faith journey, one of the biggest challenges is walking down the road with no exit in sight. An engaged woman who is abstinent until her wedding day? While I'm sure that brings about some pressures of wanting to be with the one she loves while not being able to, at least she has a date in mind, at least there is light at the end of her tunnel. But a thirty-something woman who has no idea when Mr. Right-for-Her is going to ask her to jump a broom and share a bedroom? Whew! Sometimes all you have to go on is that God knows what he's doing . . . even if you don't.

Patience with Purity

It goes without saying at this point that I'm not a virgin, but I am someone who has had her purity restored (Joel 2:25). OK, so . . . tampons. When I started having sex, let's just say I wasn't as sensitive about what I put in that sacred space. But when I decided to stop having sex, something about what a doctor said came back to me. I decided I didn't want anything else there that wasn't spiritually supposed to be. I wanted to let God and time do what he wanted to do with my womb.

A couple of months ago, I forgot about that and tried to use a light tampon. The PG version of this story is that it wasn't an easy or comfortable experience. As a woman who had no pads in the house at the time, I was irritated. As a woman who *used* to not pay the supersize ones any mind, I was ecstatic! God was restoring me. Indeed he was, and still is, preparing me for my husband.

And you know what's a trip? I was mentioning to my last sex partner, a man who is still my friend whom I love—in the right way—this revelation (yeah, I'm pretty candid across the board), and he said something so powerful. When I said, "I can't believe that sex is going to be painful again," his reply was, "Pain is always associated with a memory. You should remember giving yourself to your husband."

I should remember giving myself to my husband. I'm tearing up just thinking about it. There are many sexual acts I have done that I pray are way down deep in the sea of forgetfulness (Ps. 103:12), but there is one memory I want to hold on to for the rest of my days. It's when God gives me permission to give my mind, body, and soul to my prince. That pain will bring forth much gain.

Is that tampon thing a tip? I'd definitely do some research on the risks of tampon use. Convenient is not always better. But my bigger point is that if you really want to be made whole in this area, going to God is your first instruction. When people ask me how I got "delivered" from fornication, my response tends to be, "Deliverance, for me, is foresight." I had sex long enough to know that when I'm ovulating, I ain't nothin' to play with. When I am battling with self-esteem, calling an ex is just plain stupid. When my hormones are raging, I'm better off watching the Hallmark channel because going outside of the house, even though I am a full-grown woman, I better be on a curfew. A wise man once said that there ain't nothin' open past midnight but legs.

Yet when it comes to having patience with the process, patience with the process of God renewing you, I don't have some magic formula. All I can tell you is that it takes patience. Seemingly, a lot of people want the benefits of forgiveness without the responsibility of dealing with the consequences that come from their disobedience. Shoot, why do you think God doesn't want us caught up in the lifestyle of habitual sin to begin with? The Bible says that we will reap what we sow (Gal. 6:7–8). I don't know about you, but I don't see an expiration date on that reaping process. Repentance (remorse or contrition for past conduct or sin), true repentance is not about getting out of your consequences; it's about experiencing a mind change so that you don't create any new ones. Second Corinthians 7:10 (NKJV) says: "For godly sorrow produces repentance leading to salvation, not to be regretted; but the sorrow of the world produces death."

Godly sorrow produces repentance. Repentance leads to salvation and not only that but the kind of salvation that is not regretted. No matter what you've done in the past, *no matter what*, your sorrow can bring you to a place of repentance that will result in personal *salvation*: the preservation or deliverance from destruction, difficulty, or evil; deliverance from the power or penalty of sin; redemption.

When God Sees You . . .

As you look back over your "sex résumé," there are parts that I'm sure are going to tempt you to feel guilty, if not even a bit depressed. Don't let your anxiety about what you cannot change affect you in that way (Prov. 12:25). Romans 8:1 says that there is no condemnation in Christ, and Isaiah 1:18 assures us that if we go to God and reason with him, if we confess our sins, he will not only forgive us (1 John 1:9), but he will make us white as snow. That said, if a white wedding gown is your thing (You *do* know that's not biblical, right? It's a man-made tradition), if you've come to God in repentance—something that will reflect in your words as well as your deeds (Matt. 12:33)—no matter who knows what you used to do, or be, you can wear a white wedding gown with pride because "white as snow" is pretty darn white? *When God sees you* as pure, it doesn't matter what anyone thinks. Because when God is for you, who really can be against you (Rom. 8:31)?

However, just like so much of this journey, the body follows what the heart tells it, and so when it comes to getting your mind into a place where waiting is restoring you and not killing you, this is what I believe God gave me to share (Luke 12:12). Indeed, it's a mind-blowing blessing. As I was praying about what to say in this chapter, it was funny where God led me. During

> *When God sees you as pure, it doesn't matter what anyone thinks.*

the time of writing this piece, I was fasting with seven of my friends. The Spirit took me to Matthew 25:14–30, the story of the servants and how they invested (or failed to invest) what their master gave them. So many of us are waiting on God to do certain things for us, and yet there are "talents," resources, within our grasp to accomplish more than we think even now. What we have, for the moment is what we need. The Bible tells us so (Matt. 6:34). Use what you have wisely. However, it was right above that parable that I reread a story that I haven't thought about in at least a year or two: the five wise and five foolish virgins (the word *virgin* is used in the New King James Version).

> At that time the kingdom of heaven will be like ten brides-maids who took their lamps and went to wait for the bride-groom. Five of them were foolish and five were wise. *The five foolish bridesmaids took their lamps, but they did not take more oil for the lamps to burn. The wise bridesmaids took their lamps and more oil in jars. Because the bridegroom was late, they became sleepy and went to sleep.*

At midnight someone cried out, "The bridegroom is coming! Come and meet him!" Then all the bridesmaids woke up and got their lamps ready. But the foolish ones said to the wise, "Give us some of your oil, because our lamps are going out." The wise bridesmaids answered, "No, the oil we have might not be enough for all of us. Go to the people who sell oil and buy some for yourselves."

So while the five foolish bridesmaids went to buy oil, the bridegroom came. The bridesmaids who were ready went in with the bridegroom to the wedding feast. Then the door was closed and locked.

Later the others came back and said, "Sir, sir, open the door to let us in." But the bridegroom answered, *"I tell you the truth, I don't want to know you."*

So always be ready, because you don't know the day or the hour the Son of Man will come.

Matthew 25:1–13

Okay, you know those really good movies (like *Star Trek*) that are filled with so much information that you are scared to go to the bathroom for fear you will miss something really important? That is how this next part is going to flow: a lot of revelation without a ton of words. I think God wants it to be that way because there is a mass lesson for all of us, but based on where you are, there are some intricate things he wants to reveal to you as well.

This parable is about making sure we are ready for Christ's return, but being that the Bible so frequently compares the marriage of a man and his bride with Christ's love for the church (Eph. 5:25–27), I'm at peace with using this to illustrate another point as well.

Some years ago, I wrote an article for *Relevant* magazine about Jessica Simpson. It was during the first season of *The Newlyweds*, and I was sharing that it was obvious that being a virgin should not be the only criteria for being a "good" wife. If you make it to the wedding night that way (and God bless you *in a mighty way* if you do—that is what he created us all to do!), then you are a virgin only until consummation. However, we are called to be wives for a lifetime.

Whether it was staged or the real deal, Jessica may have not given it up before, but it appeared that she also didn't cook, clean, or budget afterward. What she *did* do was whine, pout, and nag a lot (see Prov. 21:9, 19; 25:24). I'm saying all of this to say that if you are a virgin, don't make that be a mini-god in your life. The Proverbs 31 woman had *a whole lot more going for her* than her chastity. On the other hand, if you aren't a virgin, ask God to bring you to a place of total well-being—in every room of your "house," which is just another way for saying your "temple" (1 Cor. 6:19). Just because Jessica seemingly had a successful beginning to her marriage (claimed to have remained sexually pure) doesn't mean she automatically was a great wife. She needed restoration. Holy Spirit–filled wholeness, like the virgins in Matthew 25:1–13.

Anyway, this is what we know from this passage:

- Out of ten women, five were not prepared.
- The other five actually had extra oil.
- The bridegroom was late (coming to them), and even the prepared ones fell asleep waiting.
- He came at midnight (one definition of *midnight* is "a period of intense darkness or gloom").
- The five foolish bridesmaids went to get more oil.
- The bridegroom locked them out and said (eek!), "I don't want to know you."
- The moral to the story? We must always be ready.

As bridesmaids, as single women serving and preparing, we must always be ready, for we do not know the hour that God will bless us with our groom. According to this story, it could be at one of our gloomiest points. However, here's what caused me to almost pass out. Of all of the words in this chapter, what jumped out at me the most was "oil." I wasn't sure why at first . . . until I looked up what it symbolizes in the Bible. Are you ready? It's the Holy Spirit. (Bookmark that!) The Scripture that I hold most near and dear to my heart right now is the Message version of Acts 1:7: "He told them, 'You don't get to know the time. Timing is the Father's business. What you'll get is the Holy Spirit.'"

When will our husband come? When will we get to have covenant sex? Girl, your guess is as good as mine. The timing of such things does not belong to us. *Timing is the Father's business.* But what we will get is the Holy Spirit—the oil that the five foolish bridesmaids were missing from their lamps!

Bam! These women missed out on the arrival of the bridegroom because they did not have enough of the Holy Spirit with them, the Spirit whom God sent after Christ returned home to be, catch this, please: *a Helper for us* (John 14:26 NCV and NKJV). And how did God, our Creator, describe women in the first book of the Bible? We were made to be helpers, right? Oh, how this journey has come full circle. Oh, how I pray you read this chapter at least three or four times to catch it all. The process you must be willing to subject yourself to is to love God, yourself, and your future mate enough to wait—to be patient in God's will, way, and timing. In the meantime, he didn't leave you empty-handed. He blessed you with something that is a supernatural embodiment of what he created *you* to be: a *helper.* He will support and assist you along the way, through the good times and the bad.

I pray you read this chapter three or four times to catch it all.

No wonder the Enemy hates women so! No wonder he doesn't want us to really "get it" when it comes to the reason we are here. No wonder he wants us to find words like "submit" to be worse than curse (or cuss) words. No wonder the Holy Spirit is often seen as the more feminine, in the most respectful way possible, side of God. Every day Satan sees what the Holy Spirit does in the lives of people. He can only imagine what would happen if *a person created to help* received supernatural help! Yeah, he should be scared!

So yes, through it all, we should be patient with the process. God is not taking us through this to waste time nor is he twiddling his thumbs. He is simply using these moments to make us just what he needs us to be—a physical representation of the Holy Spirit, *a helper.*

The Eulogy
of CarmaMonique
(An Alter Ego's Demise)

- - - - - - - - - - -

April 29, 2009

> A dying man needs to die, as a sleepy man needs to sleep,
> and there comes a time when it is wrong, as well as useless,
> to resist.
>
> Stewart Alsop

CarmaMonique lived her life in secret; only few knew she existed. She was birthed out of need for her companion, Candice Marie, to express herself—or who she allowed people to tell her she was. When Candice chose to deny righteousness, it was Carma who took over. On Saturday nights, Carma laid on her back in the beds of men "she" loved, while on Sunday mornings, Candice laid on her face in the house of a God who loved her, repenting. Every time she found courage to leave her "friend" behind, Carma discovered a way to play on Candice's insecurities. Candice wasn't the prettiest. Candice wasn't the skinniest. Candice wasn't the most popular. But none of that mattered with Carma. Void of inhibitions and anxieties, she became infamous. Men called Candice to speak to her. When Carma was invited over, it was Candice who was embarrassed when she thought she could stay. She initiated conversations about life and love and possibility, believing that it would encourage them to ask, "Will you be with me?" when their only question was "With or without the lights on?" Jaded by what she considered to be life's disappointments (when they were really her own), Candice Marie allowed CarmaMonique to exist daily. When Candice wrote what God spoke, Carma penned what her body craved. Instead of allowing Candice to assess what her loneliness meant, Carma called or texted or just dropped by to ensure that her leg stayed wrapped around another that night. It always amazed Candice that the "hope your day's going well" messages she sent never seemed to get a response when Carma's "same time tonight?" correspondence always secured an answer.

It wasn't until last week that the battle of coexistence began to brew. As Candice fasted from the past, Carma fought to keep it relevant. Every day that Candice rested in newfound peace, Carma wrestled with what it meant to her. It was becoming apparent that they could not occupy the same space. It had been months ago when they reached a compromise: Carma would be reintroduced on Candice's wedding night. The good girl would maneuver through society while the devious one simmered and waited her turn. But as Candice Marie learned more about herself, she realized that agreement would no longer be acceptable. For years, CarmaMonique was an extension of who Candice was but who she is now and who she plans to be will forever make them strangers. It had to end but Carma would not go quietly. "Who are you without me?" "Who will want you when they know we are not a package deal?" Those questions may have scared Candice into obedience before but not now. With five words, she took the life of the one who caused her to believe her foolish way of existence was acceptable: I want to be free.

Most eulogies speak of those who will miss the departed. The truth is, no one will miss CarmaMonique. The men in her past have not requested to be a part of Candice Marie's present, not that she would have granted it anyway. The one to whom her future belongs doesn't need to know Carma; he just needs to know she died. It was a necessary homicide that would allow him to take his bride, Candice Marie, and hold her completely—not competing with the touches and caresses of others. When he takes her, he takes her and no one else.

Their life is a united symphony that gives life to purpose, not the schizophrenic chord that sought to destroy visions before they were even dreamed. Let us not mourn CarmaMonique's life but learn from it; it is evidence that operating outside of God's perfect design will cause the counterfeit to seem authentic. It would be a lie to say that Carma is in a better place because demons do not dwell in serenity. But Candice Marie is serene, knowing that her life was spared and that is all that matters.

Live on, sistah. Live on!

Candice Marie Benbow
©BirthRight, 2009

Purity

Broken Beginnings Made Whole

Turn us back to You, O LORD, and we will be restored.

Lamentations 5:21 NKJV

The greatest gift of the garden is the restoration of the five senses.

Hanna Rion

And here we are—chapter 10. The end, but in many ways, it's also the beginning. In the Bible one of the things that the number 10 symbolizes is restoration. I don't know about you, but as I wrote this book, my mind was completely blown to see how God brought this all full circle: this book began in the Garden and now we are back where we started—prayerfully each of us is a better woman for it.

Do you recall how, in the first chapter, we spent a lot of time focusing on how we got into a broken state in the first place? How the helpmate went from being the Woman to being Eve, and how, when it comes to our sexuality, the enmity that God assured us would happen indeed did? What I also hope you witnessed was how we can be restored. The Enemy wants to destroy us, but God always provides ways for us to be redeemed.

The intro to this chapter may have caught you a bit off guard. I must admit that when I read my friend Candice's eulogy to her "stripper/whore" ego, I was both surprised and amazed. It might help to give you a little background for it all to make sense.

One day Candice and I were talking online and she said something about getting CarmaMonique ready for her future husband. My response was, "What's that? Your stripper name?" and she basically said "yes." I was half joking/half serious when I replied, "So what? Is that like a ho anointing?" Oh, what an oxymoron.

God took over from there. Earlier that day I had written a devotional message on being a "ho" versus being a housewife and why so many people, even believers, fall for the lie that we are to be "conservative" in the streets and "nasty" in the bedroom. I mean, really, why are there even words like "nasty," "dirty," or "whore" used in association with such a godly gift as sex? Why does a wife have to be anything other than a wife? Proverbs 5:15–20 tells us that to associate ourselves with the "ho spirit" is like giving a man a death sentence, literally. Oh, how sad it is that we have let the world so influence us that we want to model our sex lives after the people of the world—*when sex doesn't even belong to them.*

Candice's awesomely creative and deeply insightful words were her way of putting that demonic spirit to rest and, praise God, it was before her wedding day. Her husband doesn't need a stripper to be pleased. Proverbs 5:18 says that it is a wife who gives a husband joy. It is a wife who is to be his source or object of pleasure or satisfaction, his keen delight. She can make him happy for the rest of her days simply by being what God purposed her to be: his helper—mind, body, and spirit.

No More Bitterness

After I read her eulogy, Candice and I spent some time discussing what got us to a place where we were so spiritually schizophrenic when it came to our sexuality. One of the things we both admitted was that our tainted past had a lot to do with it. I won't speak for Candice, but as for me, it really got me thinking, both about my sexual abuse and sexual misuse.

How we are going to end this chapter is a bit different from the other ones. This will actually require your participation, more than your monetary donation to the book (thanks again) and your reading it. When I finally got to a place where I was saying, "God, I want your best for me. I don't want to live a compromised life anymore," I was startled by what he led me to do. He called me to a Past Fast.

What's that? Well, I'll explain in a minute, but for now, let me quickly express just how powerful it is if you remain open to really wanting to get free from the sins that bind you. From personal experience, I know that it can be really difficult to move into your future when you haven't fully dealt with your past. Part of the reason I was "insane" (doing the same thing while expecting a different result) is because I didn't take a time-out to really see what I was doing. The Past Fast helped me put some of the ghosts that were haunting me to rest. For me, the top three were:

1. the person who molested me
2. a guy who told me that I was too unattractive to be in his family (although for years he told me he loved me and didn't mind sleeping with me)

3. a girl who introduced me to lesbianism—probably because someone had done the same thing to her—and who was also not the nicest person I've known

For years I harbored bitterness, almost to the point of malice, against these people, but God continued to gently yet firmly reveal to me that malice is not a characteristic of a follower of Christ (1 Cor. 14:20; Eph. 4:31; Col. 3:8; 1 Peter 2:1). Yes, a part of the reason is because we are called to love even our enemies (Matt. 5:43–44), but an even greater part of the reason is because when we don't forgive, when we don't choose to release the past, it keeps us bound to the spirit of those people and what they did to us—like a sick prison sentence.

> I spent a lot of time sleeping with other people's men because of how I was introduced to sexuality. The man who molested me was married.
>
> I actually dated someone related to the guy who told me I was good enough "in the night" but not "in the day," all to prove that I was worthy of attention.
>
> I have had challenges being compassionate and forgiving toward other women most of my life because of how that girl treated me.

When I finally went to God with a sincere and contrite heart (Ps. 51:17), when I told him that I would do whatever it took to stop the cycle, to have my birthright of being a whole and complete godly woman restored, he led me to the Past Fast. As a result of it:

> I made peace with the person who molested me. I hadn't had a real conversation with him in almost fifteen years. I confronted him; he apologized. It is finished.
>
> I made peace with the guy who thought I wasn't good enough to be more than his sex partner. Now, when I

see him, I can smile. My heart is not racing and I am no longer self-conscious.

I made peace with "the girl." We haven't chatted yet, but it's all good. Timing is the Father's business, right? Right.

When I think back on Adam and Eve, I wonder what would have happened if they had gone on the Past Fast. Would Adam have changed his mind and stopped calling her "the mother of all living" and gone back to referring to her as "bone of his bone and flesh of his flesh"—the being who was taken out of him? Would there have been a way that they could feel naked and not ashamed again? One can only speculate, but what I do know for sure is that we serve a God who is faithful and he said that if we confess our sins, he will forgive us; there is no condemnation in Christ.

If you want to get back to your own personal Garden of Eden, a place where you can take dominion back in your own life, I strongly urge you to do as God suggested I do: the Past Fast. Although I am in the same status (relationally) that I was before I started this book, I can tell you that my body, mind, and spirit are not the same. My past is a part of me, but it no longer dictates the decisions that I make . . . the feelings that I have . . . the way I view myself or the world.

The purpose of a Past Fast is to break us and then restore us all at once.

This book is entitled *Pure Heart: A Woman's Guide to Sexual Integrity* because it was my prayer that once you saw just how beautiful, how special, how chosen, how sacred you really are, you wouldn't want to be a victim of self-abuse/ sexual misuse. Instead, you would want to use your body, mind, and spirit for exactly the purpose you were created—to honor God in your singleness as you prepare, if you so desire and it's within God's will (see Matt. 19:1–12 Message), for marriage.

If this is indeed your desire, then get ready to take the adventure of a lifetime. I believe (what God has shown me) the purpose of a fast from the past (Past Fast) is to break us and then restore us all at once.

Thank you for walking through this journey with me. I can't wait to hear what God does for you and through you . . . now that you are almost through (with this book)!

The Past Fast

The *past* is defined as the history of a person or nation; what has existed or has happened at some earlier time; the events, phenomena, conditions, and so on, that characterized an earlier historical period; an earlier period of a person's life that is thought to be of a shameful or embarrassing nature; no longer current; gone by; over; having served formerly in a given capacity, especially an official one; the time before the present.

To *fast* means to abstain from food, to eat sparingly or abstain from some foods. Contrary to what you may have thought, this Past Fast isn't about food, though abstaining from that which tempts our taste buds can do wonders in focusing our minds (if it didn't, God wouldn't suggest it). But this fast is more about old relationships and old sin habits from which we need to abstain for our eyes to see the truth clearly and for God to heal the broken parts of our lives. Fasting from food would provide a wonderful boost, though.

On Your Marks . . .

Sometimes, when my computer freezes and I'm too impatient to let it fix itself, I pull the plugs out of the socket. Yes, techies, I know that is not the best thing to do (patience is still something that the Godhead, through many instances in the universe, is teaching me—1 Cor. 13:4). But I think God allows such experiences to teach me a few things about what it means to let go of what's behind while reaching toward the goals that lie ahead (Phil. 3:13–15).

You see, whenever I pull the plugs, reinsert them, and then turn my computer back on, the clock on my computer goes back to 2004. The thing is, the first couple of times that I did this, I didn't even notice until I tried to log on to things like MySpace and Facebook. To my computer, those things did not exist because my clock was set before a time that they were created. The first lightbulb moment: *when you stay in the past, you don't get the benefits of the present.* It wasn't until I reset my clock that I could gain access into those websites.

Another setup for this? Through the power of the Holy Spirit (Luke 12:12), I am currently conducting (and participating in) a "Wife Curriculum" class on Facebook. Now that has been a ride! Anyway, a couple of weeks ago, I woke up with the song (see Ps. 33:3) "A Whole New World" by Peabo Bryson and Regina Belle in my head. I believe that the Holy Spirit provided it as comfort (Acts 9:31), assuring us in the class that where we desired to go (marriage) was going to be *very different* from where we have been ("singledom"). Like baptism, a wedding ceremony is the public symbolism of our desire never to be the same; the classes were/are preparing us to act accordingly.

And then, the final straw: something semi-recently happened to me that got me seething. As I was talking to a friend of mine (thanks, Trenay—Prov. 27:17), she *pulled out of me* ('cause that's really what it took) that I felt *disrespected* for one reason but *humiliated* for an entirely different one. The disrespect, which was warranted, came from the *present* situation. The humiliation attached to it came from an unresolved *past.*

Lately my life has been running in threes and so, there you go, three instances, and as they say, third time's the charm! As I spent some time in prayer about it, God, through the power of the Holy Spirit, told me: "It's time for you to go on a *Past Fast*."

Immediately, I told a few of my friends. All of them are God-seekers (and very powerful ones, at that), but none of them knew what I meant without my providing additional insights. That's one reason I know this is a very unique opportunity, but if you take part, it will do what the number 9 in the Hebrew symbolizes for you: it will make many things "complete" and "final" as far as bringing some real answers and stability into your life so that you can move into a state "exceedingly abundantly above all that we ask or think" (Eph. 3:20 NKJV).

. . . Get Set . . .

Years ago my mother gave me the li'l book *When I Loved Myself Enough* by Kim McMillen. This quote is in it: "When I loved myself enough, I learned to grieve for the hurts in life when they happen instead of making the heart heavy by lugging them around." Wise words, and an even greater confirmation for what we are about to do.

And so, if you are someone who likes living in reverse or letting the "Ghosts of Life's Past" continue to haunt you, then the Past Fast isn't for you. Carry on. But if you are one of those chosen few (Matt. 22:14) who really just wants to get on with this thing called life with as little baggage as possible (the lighter you are, the faster you can go), this will be a godsend for ya!

Let me start by saying that this is not for the bitter, manipulative, or malicious (see James 3:14–15). This fast is not to hurt people's feelings or to contradict the very thing that most of us consider ourselves to be: *disciples* (John 8:31). Furthermore, if you actually complete this and are honest—with both God and yourself—you may just be surprised how many people you find yourself reconciled to rather than leaving behind. I am currently reading a book that is "whopping me" (do you hear me?!). It's Gary Thomas's *Sacred Marriage*. Just yesterday I read:

> Christian love is displayed in loving the most difficult ones to love. . . . that's what's so difficult about Jesus' call to love others. On one level, it's easy to love God, because God doesn't smell. God doesn't have bad breath. God doesn't reward kindness with evil. God doesn't make berating comments. Loving God is *easy,* in this sense. *But Jesus really let us have it when he attached our love for God with our love for other people.*[1]

When Christ came, he said the first commandment was to love God with all of our heart, soul, and strength. The second? To love your neighbor as yourself (Luke 10:27). Therefore you can't call yourself a follower of Christ and not love those around you, *including your enemies.* As a matter of fact, the Word takes it a bit further by commanding us to love them, bless them, and pray for them (Matt. 5:43–46). The truth is, if you want to "get to them," don't "fight them" with their own weapons; they aren't used to love. Love them through their foolishness (Rom. 12:20).

So no, if you are one of those "Yeah, honey, I'm with you. I'm ready to leave some people in the dust" folks, *this fast isn't for you.* God's Word says that we are to do *nothing* out of selfish ambition, "but in lowliness of mind let each esteem others better than himself" (Phil. 2:3). That said, you actually may look up and realize that, in the effort to leave the past behind, you will be called to serve some people you least expected to serve *and* some of the least grateful/humble/likable people around. I mean, why not? *Moses did it.* Shoot, you can basically read all of Exodus to see how much of a struggle for the flesh that was!

However, if you are someone who has read and/or even quoted 2 Corinthians 5:17, I implore you to check out the verses immediately before and after:

Therefore, from now on, we regard no one according to the flesh. Even though we have known Christ according to the flesh, yet now we know Him thus no longer. Therefore, if anyone is in Christ, he is a new creation; old things have passed away; behold, all things have become new. Now all things are of God, who has reconciled us to Himself through Jesus Christ, and has given us the *ministry of reconciliation*, that is, that God was in Christ reconciling the world to Himself, not imputing their trespasses to them, and has committed to us the word of reconciliation.

2 Corinthians 5:16–19 NKJV

Through Christ, we are given the *ministry of reconciliation* and we are *committed to the word of reconciliation*. Just so we're all clear, *reconciliation* means "restoration to harmony; renewal of friendship." Likewise, *reconcile* is "to cause (a person) to accept or be resigned to something not desired, to win over to friendliness, cause to become amicable, to compose or settle (a quarrel or dispute), to bring into agreement or harmony, make compatible or consistent, to restore (an excommunicate or penitent) to communion in a church."

Yes, yes, yes. Most people want to "conveniently" (although from personal experience, I don't know how convenient it is) overlook Scripture passages like this one from 2 Corinthians. A wise man once said that just because you call a truth a lie one thousand times doesn't make it any less truthful. Applying "selective hearing" to God's Word doesn't make it any less applicable to our lives (James 1:22–24). If you claim to follow Christ, then reconciliation is not a request—it's a mandate. As a matter of fact, some of you may need to do the fast on your own next week and hold a personal "reconciliation enlightenment" fast this week on that portion of this message alone!

I'm sure you all are wondering how we can fast from the past and still be reconciled. And not only be reconciled but love our enemies. How do you move forward while there's a great chance that God will call you to minister to some of the very people you are dying to leave behind?

Good question. Immediately, when God gave me the call to fast (abstain from food), because some mountains are only moved through prayer and fasting (Matt. 17:20–21), he took me to the lead Scriptures of the fast.

Most of us are familiar with the story of Sodom and Gomorrah and how, when Lot's wife looked back (Gen. 19:26), she turned to salt. Poetic license leads me to believe that she did this because while she may have known that her home was no longer the place she needed to be, there were still things about it that she missed. And so, yes, when you think about moving away from your past and then you turn back toward something God has called you to leave, just as with Lot's wife, it has the potential to paralyze you (emotionally, mentally, physically, or even spiritually). The story of Lot's wife is a great story worth mentioning . . . because being stuck in the past is something that many people, at one point or another, struggle greatly with.

But as I was studying this story, it was actually what happened *before* that I believe we are to focus on. This is where the instruction for the Past Fast comes in. Notice how some of the lead verses are italicized? Those passages are where I will be pulling my directives. To begin this process, I encourage you to get a fresh journal and make some time to read Genesis 18 and 19 and write what God shares with you. There were some key things that jumped out at me when I read them, but there may be some things that he'll share with you as it relates to your own personal journey.

. . . Go!

We will use the story about Lot and his family to guide us through the process of the Past Fast.

But the two men staying with Lot opened the door, pulled him back inside the house, and then closed the door. *They struck those outside the door with blindness, so the men, both young and old, could not find the door.*

The two men said to Lot, "Do you have any other relatives in this city? Do you have any sons-in-law, sons, daughters, or any other relatives? If you do, tell them to leave now, because we are about to destroy this city. The LORD has heard of all the evil that is here, so he has sent us to destroy it."

So Lot went out and said to his future sons-in-law who were pledged to marry his daughters, "Hurry and leave this city! The LORD is about to destroy it!" But they thought Lot was joking.

At dawn the next morning, the angels begged Lot to hurry. They said, "Go! Take your wife and your two daughters with you so you will not be destroyed when the city is punished."

But Lot delayed. So the two men took the hands of Lot, his wife, and his two daughters and led them safely out of the city. So the LORD was merciful to Lot and his family. After they brought them out of the city, one of the men said, "Run for your lives! Don't look back or stop anywhere in the valley. Run to the mountains, or you will be destroyed."

But Lot said to one of them, "Sir, please don't force me to go so far! You have been merciful and kind to me and have saved my life. *But I can't run to the mountains.* The disaster will catch me, and I will die. Look, that little town over there is not too far away. Let me run there. It's really just a little town, and I'll be safe there."

The angel said to Lot, "Very well, I will allow you to do this also. I will not destroy that town. But run there fast, because *I cannot destroy Sodom until you are safely in that town.*" (That town is named Zoar, because it is little.)

Genesis 19:10–22

1. THE ATTACK

They struck those outside the door with blindness, so the men, both young and old, could not find the door (Gen.

19:11). If you read all of Genesis 19, you will see that there were two men (angels) who came to Sodom. The city was so evil that men living there came to Lot's house because they heard that there was "fresh meat" in town (no joke—check the story) and they wanted to have their way with the men. They demanded it, actually. When Lot offered up his daughters instead (what?!), the men tried to break into his house. The angels pulled Lot in and then struck those who were trying to attack the home with blindness so they could not find the door.

Instruction: In your fresh *journal (that means one you have never written in before), ask God to reveal to you the things that are trying to attack your body, mind, and spirit. Then ask God to provide you with Scripture that speaks against those things.* Some great ones for starters are Psalm 139:14; Proverbs 3:6; 4:23; Jeremiah 17:9; 31:3; Matthew 7:6; John 14:26; Romans 8:36–40; 1 Corinthians 6:18–20; 10:13; 2 Corinthians 5:17; James 1:5; and 2 Timothy 1:7.

You see, here's the thing. Many of us live in our own "Sodom" and we are afraid to leave. For some of us, it's because, even though it's been evil, it's home for us. But for even more, it's because there are spirits that have been threatening to attack us if we try to leave. Some of us want to get married, but we are afraid that we will end up just like our parents. Some of us want to have children, but we're still grieving our past miscarriages and abortions. Some of us want to start a new career, but we keep remembering botching up the last three companies we started. The spirits are banging at our doors, but instead of going to God about them, asking him to surround us with his angels and to blind the spirits so they can't find our heart's door, we are actually talking to the spirits, pleading with them as if they have a heaven or hell to put us in.

Just as God did for Job (Job 1:9–11), God has a hedge around us as well (please believe it), but I think sometimes we forget that. Ask God to, in some way, reveal his heavenly hedge that is protecting you from the things that threaten to attack you—the things in the "City of the Past" that you have been terrified to leave. Then have the courage to leave and, as you do, guard yourself from the temptation of looking backward like Lot's wife did.

2. The Urgency

Do you have any other relatives in this city? Do you have any sons-in-law, sons, daughters, or any other relatives? If you do, tell them to leave now, because we are about to destroy this city. The LORD has heard of all the evil that is here, so he has sent us to destroy it (Gen. 19:12–13). I am telling you that just as there was a sense of urgency with Lot and his family, there is one for you now. The past mentality that many of us are in is pure evil and counterproductive. We must leave it behind.

But does that mean we leave everything in it behind as well? A while back, Vince Gill wrote the song "Which Bridge to Cross and Which Bridge to Burn." Seemingly, that is one of life's greatest challenges: deciding between the two. But because being a disciple also means that we are called to *reconciliation*, and since believers are brothers and sisters in Christ, before leaving your past behind, make a plea to those in it. Yes, you are moving forward, but you should love others enough to want to bring them with you (because God wants to renew more than just you).

> As Christ-followers, we have a duty to invite others to a better life.

The catch is that you are about to become a new person. *Old things will have passed away* (2 Cor. 5:17 NKJV). This means you don't want to discuss your past (within reason, because some of you need to apologize and repent for what you did in the past—see Matt. 5:23–24); you don't want to relive your past; you no longer want to do any or all of the things that the past person did. You are going forward.

Now here's the other catch: you don't have time to cry, beg, plead, and justify this decision. Either the people you invite are going to come . . . or they're not. But as Christ-followers, we have a *duty* to invite others to a better life.

Instruction: Pray for those you have known in this "past–present" life of yours.

Don't just pray for the people you *like*, pray for everyone. And, as God leads, go to them either by phone, by email, over lunch—through some kind of direct contact—and tell them of your decision to let God destroy the past that you have been living in and share with them your desire for your present. This is another reason you will need a journal, because your thoughts/words need to be very clear and concise (Matt. 5:37). Write out in your journal what you want to say.

If you don't want to get drunk anymore, then tell the people you used to get drunk with that they can no longer drink around you. Period. Nonnegotiable.

If you don't want to gossip, tell the people you used to gossip with that they don't need to bring other people up around you. Period. Nonnegotiable.

If you don't want to get into arguments anymore (why, oh why, do we miss how biblical *that* is—Phil. 2:14), tell the people you used to argue with that you will not allow them to pull you out of your comfort zone and violate your boundaries anymore. Period. Nonnegotiable.

Do you see what God is doing? He is not freeing us so much from people but from the spirits within them. How dare we think, when God gave us his Son for the sake of our lives (John 10:10), that we have the right to abandon, ignore, or excommunicate *anyone* from our lives. *They have the choice to stay or leave, on our godly terms.* By setting new boundaries, we have a very similar opportunity to that which Lot had: "I am leaving who I was and I would love for you to join me with who I am becoming, but you will have to leave who you were behind as well, or this can't happen."

Some people will think you are kidding. That's on them. But God is ready to do a new thing, and I promise you that as I live, breathe, and type this in the wee hours of the morning, *now* it shall spring forth (Isa. 43:19). You will see how many people want to live in the new by how they react and respond to the new boundaries you set.

3. Don't Delay

But Lot delayed. So the two men took the hands of Lot, his wife, and his two daughters and led them safely out of the city. So the LORD was merciful to Lot and his family. After they brought them out of the city, one of the men said, "Run for your lives! Don't look back or stop anywhere in the valley. Run to the mountains, or you will be destroyed" (Gen. 19:16–17).

Don't delay the act of reconciliation, of fasting from the past. Your delay is keeping you from all that God has for you. Many of us quote 1 Corinthians 2:9 (NKJV), "Eye has not seen, nor ear heard, nor have entered into the heart of man, the things which God has prepared for those who love Him." But I am going to be honest with you: the closer I get to God, the more I see and hear about what he has in store for me (Jer. 33:3; James 1:5).

Some of you think you are waiting on God, when actually God is waiting on you. He's not going to give you a new husband when you are hung up on your old boyfriend. He's not going to give you a job when you are still attached to the old city you live in. He's not going to give you new responsibilities while you continue to cling to your old habits.

God will lead you out of your past, but you have to be willing to do some of the work as well. You see how Lot and his family were instructed: "Run for your lives! Don't look back or stop anywhere in the valley." This can be seen to parallel the following Scriptures:

> *Flee* sexual immorality. Every sin that a man does is outside the body, but he who commits sexual immorality sins against his own body.
>
> 1 Corinthians 6:18 NKJV

> Therefore, my beloved, *flee* from idolatry.
>
> 1 Corinthians 10:14 NKJV

> For the love of money is a root of all kinds of evil, for which some have strayed from the faith in their greediness, and pierced themselves through with many sorrows. But you, O man of God, *flee* these things and pursue righteousness, godliness, faith, love, patience, gentleness. Fight the good fight of faith, lay hold on eternal life, to which you were also called and have confessed the good confession in the presence of many witnesses.
>
> 1 Timothy 6:10–12 NKJV

> *Flee* also youthful lusts; but *pursue* righteousness, faith, love, peace with those who call on the Lord out of a pure heart.
>
> 2 Timothy 2:22 NKJV

Instruction: Make these your meditation Scriptures for the week.

To flee something is to move swiftly away from it. If you really want to leave your past, you will flee from anything that ties you to it. If you want to be able to discern who desires to leave your past with you, watch the lifestyle of that person. *New creations* don't desire to be sexually immoral. *New creations* don't revel in idolatry. *New creations* are not driven by money at all costs. *New creations* make it a daily pursuit to live in righteousness, faith, love, and peace.

4. Make the Needed Adjustments

But I can't run to the mountains (Gen. 19:19). Now, I'm going to take a little bit of poetic license. I'm sure that the angels wanted Lot to run to the mountains so that he could be as far away from the "fire damage" as possible. I'm not sure if it was his age, fear, attachment, or all of the above that made Lot decline the *first instruction* (something I try not to do with God . . . anymore), but I'm here to encourage you not to do what Lot did.

God is going to call some of us to run to the mountains of our faith to get as far away from our past as possible. (Speaking of mountains, did you see that "Zoar" was called that because it was *little*? God's call is often greater than what we settle for or think in our own power that we can accomplish.) Climbing a mountain is hard work; the atmosphere is different up there. But if God calls you to do it, go and pray, "LORD, by Your favor You have made my mountain stand strong" (Ps. 30:7 NKJV). You see, here's the thing: weak mountain climbers don't exist. There is a certain endurance that is needed to reach the top of your personal mountain but you can be sure that if God called you to it, he will give you the strength to overcome. As you leave your past, God will be using this time to "work out" some things. It's very difficult to go into something new if you haven't changed. Leaving is not enough. You have to be open to making some internal adjustments as well.

> *God will lead you out of your past, but you have to be willing to do some of the work as well.*

Instruction: James 5:16 tells us that it is in confessing our faults that we find healing. On a sheet of paper, write down the things inside of you that cause you to fear. Get an accountability partner to pray for/with you concerning these things. At the end of your fast, burn that list.

My personal journey has revealed to me that I can't love God, myself, or my neighbor when fear is in the way (1 John 4:18). Are you still living in lies and secrecy because you are scared to face the truth? Are you not giving during this recession because you are scared that you won't have enough to meet your own needs (see Luke 6:38)? Are you unwilling to draw some clear lines in your romantic relationship because you are scared that you will lose the person? This is what mountain-moving faith is all about. This is also why we are fasting. If, in leaving your past, God calls you to do some uncomfortable things for the purpose of increasing your faith and refining your character (Rom. 5:3–5), *do them!* Nothing with God is for naught (Matt. 10:39).

5. LEAVE THE PAST BEHIND

I cannot destroy Sodom until you are safely in that town (Gen. 19:22). God cannot destroy the hindrances of our past until we leave them behind, until we *abstain* from them, as the definition of "fast" implies.

We have heard that God hates the sin and not the sinner and that still stands true. And for the sake of us all, may I just say, "Thank you, Lord!" For instance, some of us are wondering why our divorce still feels like an open wound, why we can recall the abuse from our father's hand like it was yesterday, why our sinful acts in college still spiritually (not all spirits are good spirits) stalk us. It's because we are still an active participant in our past. We still talk about it. We still give it top priority attention. We still let people keep us in it, like, "Girl, do you still hang out with so-and-so? I remember when you used to do such-and-such."

God won't remove the past from us until we make the decision that we want it to be removed. It has to work that way, because if he destroyed those things *now*, before we are ready, it would hurt us in the process. *Hurting us is never God's initial desire.* In Genesis 18:17–33 Abraham pled with God not to destroy Sodom if God could find even ten good people in it. God agreed; he was willing to spare an entire city for *ten people*. God is not in the people-destroying business, just the sin-destroying business. Sometimes that means both have to go, but his merciful Spirit is patient (Luke 6:36). He wants to remove your past (and the pain that comes with it) from you. But you have to want that first. Get your body, mind, and spirit out of the past so that he can fix it to where it will not affect you in the same way ever again.

Instruction: Get a purpose plan together of where you desire to go. This week, ask God to show you a new place—a river in the desert, so to speak—that can give you a comfort, a hope, a new burst of energy so that what you are leaving pales in comparison to where you are headed.

Any therapist worth his or her credentials will tell you that you can't get rid of something effectively unless you are prepared to replace it with something else. If your job is your "Sodom," when you quit, what are you going to do? If your fetish is your "Sodom," when you let it go, what are you going to do with that extra time on your hands (see Prov. 19:15)? If your past friends are your "Sodom," isolation is not the way to deal with the initial loneliness that comes with leaving them behind.

God is not in the people-destroying business, just the sin-destroying business.

There's no real point in leaving something unless you have something to go to. The Israelites left Egypt for the Promised Land. Lot left Sodom for the town of Zoar. Ruth left Moab for Bethlehem. Esther left the comforts of her home for the palace. In all of these instances, people left something behind, but also in all of these instances, they had, through God's unction, a place to go in mind.

Some of us have a hard time leaving our past because we don't have a clue what we are leaving it for. We know it's bad but at least it's familiar. God wants to bring so much into our lives, but so many of us already have too much cluttering up our heart/mind/soul space. To make room for something new, there needs to be room, right? We must get to cleanin'.

Bonus instruction: For the next seven days, *have absolutely no contact with anything tied to your past that you deem unhealthy (not uncomfortable but unhealthy). For some of you this will be people, but for more of you it will be the music you listen to, the shows you watch, the places you go (because of the spirits that are there), and the types of conversations you have—anything that feeds into a "past mentality" psyche. If these things are attached to your work, then make the interaction as limited as possible! For instance, if you want to be freed from lust, then don't speak to any of the past "lust people" you were involved with (it's hard to see something new when something old is blocking your space). I think you get my drift.*

If you stick it out, a new thing—a new thing indeed—is waiting for you on the other side of next week: "People in the land who ask for blessings will ask for them from the faithful God. And people in the land who make a promise will promise in the name of the faithful God, because the troubles of the past will be forgotten. I will make those troubles go away" (Isa. 65:16).

A New Time Is Coming

Look, I will make new heavens and a new earth, and people will not remember the past or think about those things. My people will be happy forever because of the things I will make. I will make a Jerusalem that is full of joy, and I will make her people a delight.

Isaiah 65:17–18

Amen . . . amen . . . and amen again!

For all the promises of God in Him *are* Yes, and in Him Amen, to the glory of God through us.

1 Corinthians 1:20 NKJV

It is finished. Your life, as a *woman*, has begun.

Afterword

When I finish reading a book, one of two things usually happens. I either toss it on the shelf or I give it away. But something different happened when I read this one. I put it on my desk in a place where I could easily reach it. I want access to it because of how often women approach me to ask for help with their porn problem.

I always send a woman to counsel a woman. As I continue to craft this ministry, I need an influential voice like Shellie's close at hand. Since we started XXXchurch, the parameters and rules of the game have changed. Porn producers are not fighting fair. Instead, they continue to exploit the hurting, abandoned, neglected, and alone. Even the girls in porn are becoming wise to the game. In a recent VH1 episode of *Sex Rehab*, a woman porn star summed it up: "I'm a monster." She was describing the shame and guilt she felt because of how she had used her body to exploit people.

In chapter 2, Shellie summed up the entire purpose of XXXchurch: "*I know God had more in mind for my sex life than physical pleasure. He wanted my soul to have peace; he wanted my emotions to be tended to; he wanted my mind to be at rest. . . . He wanted me to have sex with a purpose.*"

Find your purpose.

Find your peace.

God is not mad at you. He is mad about you. He created you to love and be loved. You are priceless. You are his chosen princess. As the Father, he sees you as *Daddy's little girl*. Let those words rescue you.

As you continue your journey, take advantage of the tools and resources around you. If you have not done so, visit us online at www.XXXchurch.com and dive into free software, an accountability relationship, and an ongoing curriculum that will help your pursuit of wholeness.

Shellie writes a blog for women every week on the site. Take advantage of these resources; you'll be glad you did.

Continue the journey and make sure to tell us of the changes you have made because of the hope you have found.

We believe in you.

Craig Gross

Notes

Chapter 2 Sex

1. Tim Alan Gardner, *Sacred Sex* (Colorado Springs: Waterbrook, 2002), 23.

Chapter 3 Sexual Additives, Part One

1. Centers for Disease Control and Prevention, http://www.cdc.gov/nchs/nsfg/abc_list_s.htm#oralsexmalefemale.
2. Paul O'Malley, http://www.cdc.gov/nchs/nsfg/abc_list_s.htm.

Chapter 4 Sexual Additives, Part Two

1. Jerry Ropelato, "Internet Pornography Statistics," Internet-Filter-Review.com, http://internet-filter-review.toptenreviews.com/internet pornography-statistics.html.
2. Ibid.
3. Brigham Young University, "National Pornography Statistics," http://wsr.byu.edu/content/national-pornography-statistics.
4. Ibid.
5. Ibid.
6. *Today's Christian Woman*, fall 2003, in http://www.safefamilies.org/sfStats.php.

7. DivorceWizards.com and Jennifer Schneider, *Cybsersex Exposed: Simple Fantasy or Obsession?* on http://www.lightedcandle.org/pornstats/stats.asp.

8. Brigham Young University, "National Pornography Statistics."

Chapter 5 Overexposure

1. "The Body Shop," *Essence*, June 2009.

2. B. S. Greenberg and M. G. Woods, "The soaps: Their sex, gratifications, and outcomes," *Journal of Sex Research* 36 (1999): 250–57, http://www.soc.ucsb.edu/sexinfo/article/sexuality-in-the-mass-media; and the Kaiser Family Foundation, "Sex on TV: Content and Context:

A Biennial Report to the Kaiser Family Foundation," http://www.kff.org/entmedia/upload/Sex-on-TV-A-Biennial-Report-to-the-Kaiser-Family-Foundation-1999-Report.pdf.

Chapter 10 Purity

1. Gary Thomas, *Sacred Marriage* (Grand Rapids: Zondervan, 2000), 42.

Resources

Online

www.XXXchurch.com
www.x3pure.com (30 days to purity workshop)
www.everymansbattle.com
www.purelifeministries.org
www.higher-calling.com
www.sash.net (Society for the Advancement of Sexual Health)
www.slaafws.org (Sex and Love Addicts Anonymous)
www.sexhelp.com (Dr. Patrick Carnes Sexual Addiction Resources)

Recommended Reading

Anger: Handling a Powerful Emotion in a Healthy Way by Gary Chapman
Finding Favor with the King by Tommy Tenney
The Five Love Languages (Singles Edition) by Gary Chapman
Forgiveness: Breaking the Power of the Past by Kay Authur, David Lawson, and BJ Lawson

The Gospel of Ruth by Carolyn Custis James
Healed Without Scars by David G. Evans
It's Not About Me by Max Lucado
Lady in Waiting by Jackie Kendall and Debby Jones
Love & Respect by Dr. Emerson Eggerichs
Prayer by Richard J. Foster
Real Christianity by William Wilberforce
Redeeming Love by Francine Rivers
Sacred Influence by Gary Thomas
Sacred Marriage by Gary Thomas
Sacred Sex by Tim Alan Gardner
Safe People by Henry Cloud and John Townsend
Saving Your Marriage Before It Starts by Les and Leslie
   Parrott
Sex God by Rob Bell
Single, Married, Separated and Life After Divorce by Myles
   Monroe
Understanding the Purpose and Power of Woman by Myles
   Monroe

Other Resources

Recovery

Arterburn, Stephen. *Every Man's Battle: Winning the War
   on Sexual Temptation One Victory at a Time.* Colorado
   Springs: WaterBrook, 2000.

Arterburn, Stephen, Fred Stoeker, and Mike Yorkey. *Every
   Heart Restored: A Wife's Guide to Healing in the Wake of
   a Husband's Sexual Sin.* Colorado Springs: WaterBrook,
   2004.

Black, Claudia, PhD. *It Will Never Happen to Me: Growing
   Up with Addiction as Youngsters, Adolescents, Adults.*
   Center City, MN: Hazelden, 2001.

Carnes, Patrick, PhD. *Facing the Shadow: Starting Sexual and Relationship Recovery*, 2nd ed. Carefree, AZ: Gentle Path Press, 2008.

Carnes, Patrick, Debra Laaser, and Mark Laaser. *Open Hearts: Renewing Relationships with Recovery, Romance and Reality*. Carefree, AZ: Gentle Path Press, 1999.

Earle, Ralph H., and Mark R. Laaser. *The Pornography Trap: Setting Pastors and Laypersons Free from Sexual Addiction*. Kansas City: Beacon Hill Press, 2002.

Gallagher, Steve. *Out of the Depths of Sexual Sin*. Dry Ridge, KY: Pure Life Ministries, 2003.

Maltz, Wendy, and Larry Maltz. *The Porn Trap: The Essential Guide to Overcoming Problems Caused by Pornography*. New York: HarperCollins, 2008.

Schnarch, David. *Intimacy and Desire*. New York: Beaufort Books, 2009.

Faith

Answers in the Heart: Daily Meditations for Men and Women Recovering from Sex Addiction. Center City, MN: Hazelden, 1989.

Gross, Craig. *Dirty Little Secret*. Grand Rapids: Zondervan, 2006.

Hope and Recovery: The Twelve-Step Guide for Healing from Compulsive Sexual Behavior. Center City, MN: Hazelden, 1994.

Nouwen, Henri. *Reaching Out: The Three Movements of the Spiritual Life*. Garden City, NY: Doubleday, 1986.

_____. *The Return of the Prodigal Son: A Story of Homecoming*. New York: Doubleday, 1986.

Palmer, Parker J. *A Hidden Wholeness: The Journey toward an Undivided Life*. San Francisco: John Wiley and Sons, 2004.

_____. *Let Your Life Speak: Listening for the Voice of Vocation*. San Francisco: John Wiley and Sons, 1999.

Software

Accountability Software: X3watch, www.x3watch.com
Internet Filtering Software: Safe Eyes, www.safeeyes.com/
xxxchurch

Recovery Groups

Celebrate Recovery, www.celebraterecovery.com
LIFE Ministries, www.freedomeveryday.org
Sexaholics Anonymous, www.sa.org
Sex Addicts Anonymous, www.saa-recovery.org

Live-in Programs

Pure Life Ministries, www.purelifeministries.org
Bethesda Workshops, www.bethesdaworkshops.org

Serenity Prayer

God, grant me the Serenity
To accept the things I cannot change . . .
Courage to change the things I can,
And Wisdom to know the difference.

Living one day at a time,
Enjoying one moment at a time,
Accepting hardship as the pathway to peace.
Taking, as He did, this sinful world as it is,
Not as I would have it.
Trusting that He will make all things right
if I surrender to His will.
That I may be reasonably happy in this life,
And supremely happy with Him forever in the next.
Amen.

Reinhold Niebuhr

Acknowledgments

Thank you to . . .

My parents, Eugene Warren and Gail Masondo, for loving me through the process and for giving me such a beautiful name: Shellie, which means "mine, belonging to me"; Renee means "reborn"; and Warren means "loyal; protector." I hope I've done the legacy proud and I love you for loving me in the special way that you do.

"Baba" Victor Masondo for being a wonderful man and an awesome mentor. I adore you.

Jonathan Christian "Ziyon" Hamilton for being the best brother a girl could have and the best kind of friend I would ever want (next to my future husband . . . and God, of course!). *Love* ain't a strong enough word for how I feel about you.

To the rest of my blood family. We've got to do better on the communication thing. Life is short, but thanks for the DNA . . . and prayers. Truly, madly, deeply.

My (big and little) spiritual sisters who *consistently*, in this season, hold me down like nobody's business: Marcella Watts, Tia Mitchell, Trenay Bynum, Carmen Starling, Adrianne Grant, Shauna Randolph, LaShawn Williams,

Wanda Ramsey, Anastasia Nocentelli, Regina Enochs, Angie Hinds, Sharon Johnson, Rachel Hockett, Hattie Winston Wheeler, Gwen Brown, and Phonethip Liu.

My, what I call, "Love Brothers," who protect me, check me, and love me in a way only they can. You have restored me in ways that my future husband will thank you for in years to come: Joey Richey, Shannon Sanders, Keith Jones, Kellye Hawkins, Anthonol Neely, Stanley Fields, James Randolph, Harold Wheeler, Jim Chaffee, Damien Horne, Brian Jones (Nashville), and Brian Hockett.

The "assigned" wives who are praying for me. You know who you are and I am praying for God to bless all of your marriages TENFOLD.

The "One Fire" women who have made Facebook a joy and not a chore. Thank you.

The couples who have given me TMI in order that I won't have to send up SOS signals in my own marriage someday. I'm sure you would rather remain anonymous. I get it and I thank you.

The following people for their consistent (can you tell "consistent" is a big word for me these days?), random, "right on time" support and/or words of encouragement: Molly Secours, Tasha Simone, Laura Lasky, Drew Ramsey, Mario Nocentelli, Joelle Dussek, Gerard Gold, Claudia Harmon, Toye Collins, the Orrs, Rashad the Poet, Sarah Gaines, Lisa Jordan, Denise Randolph, Jackie Conley, Dwann Holmes Olsen, Sandy BeCoats, Louis Upkins, Brandi Sellerz Jackson, Tara Holt, La-Drena Bolden, A. Denise Henderson, Jennifer Dye, Toya Haynes, Kenitra Woods, Rissi Palmer, Candice Marie Benbow, and Ron Wynn.

The man who is teaching me more about love than I would have ever expected to learn or experience. "Tamer," you know who you are. You've changed my life and my heart—for the better. Thank you.

The authors whose influence (via their books) prepared me for this book: Tim Alan Gardner, Francine Rivers, Gary Thomas, Barbara Pine, James Redfield, Iyanla Vanzant, Henry Cloud, John Townsend, C. S. Lewis, and William Wilberforce.

My li'l "love" nieces and nephews who bring Isaiah 54 to life for me: Re'gine, Jessica, Jasmine, Chase, Shiloh, Sarai, Zion, Ty, Taj, Zeboreh, Ruby Grace, Caroline Irene, Nia, Akello, Amina, the li'l Miss Robinsons, Olivia Grace, Caydence . . . and the many others on the way.

The Youth for Christ (Nashville) family for being the answer to a prayer regarding having my territory expanded and to all of my "daughters" who have given me "granddaughters" way before my years. You are a manifestation of restoration from my past choices re: pregnancy. *Thank you.*

XXXchurch for not only letting me be myself but for boldly encouraging my distinctiveness. Especially Michelle and Craig. God definitely makes room for people's gifts. Thanks, Craig, for opening the door and, Michelle, for making it a pleasant place to stay once I entered.

And finally, to all those, both friend and foe, who taught me more lessons than I would've thought a woman in her thirties needed in one lifetime. I once read an "author unknown" quote which so poignantly stated, "What you love, you empower, and what you fear, you empower, and what you empower, you attract." When you think about it, that means that *every single person I have encountered*, I can and should thank for bringing me to this place. I've heard that you are what you attract and I am on the constant pursuit of being (and attracting) love. For those who remain in the past, thanks for the memories; for those staying in my present, thanks for the company; and for those who will be a part of my future, thanks for the commitment.

Shellie R. Warren is an author, public speaker, and the co-ordinator for teen moms for the local chapter of a national nonprofit in Nashville, Tennessee. She is the author of *Inside of Me: Lessons of Lust, Love and Redemption* and has been published in numerous publications including *Women's Health & Fitness*, *Upscale*, *CCM*, and *Relevant*. Warren is also the founder of ButterflyAngel.org, an organization for survivors of sexual abuse and misuse; the author of two feature blogs for single women who desire to be married—sohowdidyouknow.blogspot.com and beforeyoujumpthe broom.blogspot.com; and a featured blogger and speaker for XXXchurch.com.

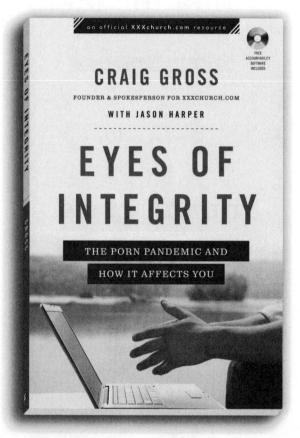

An Open, Honest, and Biblically Based Guide for Men

When it comes to sex and sexuality, men often find themselves in a losing battle against temptation. Craig Gross and Steven Luff offer men an honest look at an uncomfortable issue that will free them to experience forgiveness and renewal.

Go to XXXchurch.com for the tools
you need to respond to the porn pandemic.
These resources, specifically designed for
individuals, couples, families, and churches,
are not available anywhere else.

This website is updated daily with helps and resources for parents, women, men, youth, spouses, pastors, and more. Join the discussion! **www.xxxchurch.com**

Free accountability software available from XXXchurch or with purchase of *Eyes of Integrity*. This software automatically emails a selected accountability partner whenever a questionable internet site has been accessed. This information is meant to encourage open and honest conversation between friends and help us all be more accountable. **www.x3watch.com**

Offers 30-day online workshops featuring Steven Luff and Shellie R. Warren. These frank and open discussions are excellent companions to *Pure Eyes* and *Pure Heart*. **www.x3pure.com**

Discover the amazing love Jesus has for you.

No matter who you are, what you've done, or where you're going, Jesus loves you with a fierce and undiluted love. And he calls you to love others in the same way.

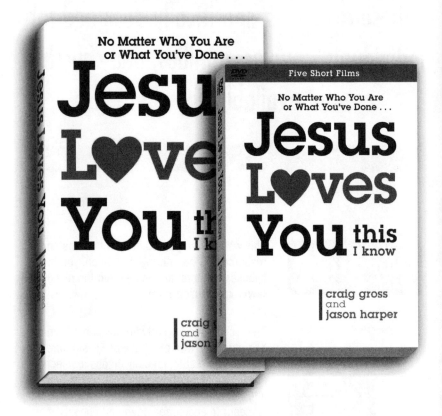

"The story of Jesus' love never gets old, and in these stories it is even newer and more beautiful and transforming than ever."—Shauna Niequist, author of *Cold Tangerines*

Don't miss the Jesus Loves You DVD and website! www.jesuslovesyou.net